NAKSHATRAS

INDIA · SINGAPORE · MALAYSIA

NAKSHATRAS

The Journey of Soul

PART 2

HIMANSHU SHANGARI

INDIA • SINGAPORE • MALAYSIA

Notion Press

No.8, 3rd Cross Street,
CIT Colony, Mylapore,
Chennai, Tamil Nadu – 600004

First Published by Notion Press 2020
Copyright © Himanshu Shangari 2020
All Rights Reserved.

ISBN 978-1-63633-584-1

OM NAMAH SHIVAAY

This book has become possible with the Grace of Lord Shiva and each valuable word in it is only due to his Blessings. This Book is dedicated to the advancement of study of Vedic Astrology.

OM NAMAH SHIVAAY

Contents

They Come First

After bowing to Lord Shiva, let me take this moment to bow to the person who has been a very strong and supportive influence in my life. She is my respected and adorable mother, **Smt. Jeewan Lata**. So much can be said about her contribution to my life, that a whole book can be written about it. However, I will simply say that even an ocean of words can't describe her true contribution to my life.

After that, I bow to my dear and respected father **Lt. Sh. Bodh Raj Shangari**. Though he left us when I was nine only, the mere fact that he along with my mother brought me to this world, makes me indebted to him for this life as well as for the lives to come. God bless your soul father, wherever you are! Though you are physically not with me, you are always there with me and in me, through all the sweet memories of my childhood, and you will always be.

Prelude

Vedic astrology is a very old and comprehensive faith of astrology. Though some other similar faiths are like streams or rivers, Vedic astrology is an ocean which can provide resources to many of these faiths. I have studied and researched many such faiths like Numerology and Vastu but none of them holds its ground without the support of Vedic astrology. It is the faith which is the backbone of many such faiths. This is what inspired me to make a carrier choice with the ocean itself. After years and years of this voyage; I can happily say that I made the right choice.

The fact that Vedic astrology is among the oldest faiths of its kind, also makes it vulnerable to many types of corruptions and adulterations from time to time. Some of these adulterations may be the results of misinterpretations of various concepts of Vedic astrology from time to time. Some others may be there because some scholars may have twisted some definitions, for selfish motives. Due to such adulterations, corruptions and misinterpretations, Vedic astrology may not look as capable and accurate to a number of people, as it actually is.

With the grace of Lord Shiva, I have spent years in researching various concepts of Vedic astrology. It has been a constant effort to find out where and how much, such concepts may have been misinterpreted; and what could be the correct interpretations of these concepts. Though in their misinterpreted forms, most such concepts of Vedic astrology don't hold ground in real practice of astrology, almost all of them hold solid ground in their modified forms. This effort has taken many years of research and analysis of thousands of horoscopes. The results however, have been very rewarding.

This book is an effort to create awareness among the lovers of Vedic astrology that this faith is still as capable as it was when it was born. Various misinterpretations from time to time may have caused confusions related to many important concepts of this faith. Through this book, an attempt has been made to create awareness about the concept of nakshatras. They deal with the finest aspects of Vedic astrology. Hence they add that leading edge to the readings; many astrologers may be looking for.

The playground for all astrological entities is taken as circular; which includes movement within a range of 360 degrees. This playground is further divided into 12 zones which are called zodiac signs and each zone or zodiac sign owns 30 degrees. These zodiac signs keep appearing on the sky of a particular location, one after another, in cyclic pattern.

While one of these signs takes lead at a time; the others assume different positions or angles, according to a fixed pattern. This way, each sign gets to be the leader for about two hours and a cycle is completed in about 24 hours. The sign which appears as the leader on the sky of a particular place at the time of birth of a native; represents the first house of his horoscope. Hence this sign becomes his ascendant or Lagna.

Horoscopes are also divided into twelve houses with each house enclosing 30 degrees, just like signs. If Aries is the rising sign at the time of birth of a native, it is assigned to the first house. It means Aries becomes the ascendant of such horoscope. The next sign Taurus is assigned to the second house and this process goes on, completing at the twelfth house being assigned to the twelfth sign Pisces.

At any given point in time, each planet among navagraha is transiting through a zodiac sign. The movement of these planets also happens to be cyclic. Once the sign representing the ascendant as well as those representing the other houses of a horoscope are found, the planets are assigned to various houses; according to their transits in various signs at that time.

This is the bigger setup through which a horoscope works. However, there is a finer setup which works within this bigger setup. This finer setup is used to calculate finer results and this setup is represented by nakshatras. According to this finer setup, the playground is further divided into 27 sub zones called nakshatras, with each one of them claiming 13 degrees and 20 minutes; amounting to a total of 360 degrees. Each subzone further contains 4 finer zones called four quarters or padas of a nakshatra, with each one of them claiming 3 degrees and 20 minutes.

This way, the playground is divided into 108 finer divisions, with 4 divisions for each one of 27 nakshatras. These 108 finer divisions again add up to 360 degrees. Since each sign contains 30 degrees, it means it contains 9 of such 108 finer divisions called navamshas. The word navamsha literally means the ninth part of something, which in this context means ninth part of a sign. Nine multiplied by 3 degrees and 20 minutes gives 30 degrees and 108 multiplied by 3 degrees and 20 minutes gives 360 degrees; which solves the equation perfectly.

The journey from Aries to Pisces and the journey from Ashwini to Revati is the journey of liberation, as we will try to find out through this series of books. The first two nakshatras Ashwini and Bharani falling in Aries deal more with the early stages of evolution. On the other hand, the last two nakshatras Uttarabhadrapada and Revati falling in Pisces deal more with the final stages of evolution.

Between the beginning and completion of this journey, each soul crosses many levels and stages of evolution; represented by different nakshatras. Through this book, we will try to understand the role of different nakshatras in shaping our personalities as well as in indicating our stages of evolution at the beginning of various lives that we assume. This book features the last 13 nakshatras from Swati to Revati.

Lord Shiva Bless You

Himanshu Shangari

Swati

Swati is 15th among 27 nakshatras. All four quarters of Swati fall in Libra. The literal meaning of the word Swati is 'independent' or 'self-going'. Vedic astrology translates the meaning of this word as independent, delicate and self-going.

Each of these seemingly different meanings of the word Swati has its influence on Swati. Vedic astrology assigns a young plant-shoot being blown by the wind, as the main symbol of Swati. The young stage of the plant-shoot represents its delicate stage. Hence delicate becomes a characteristic of Swati. The action of strong wind on the young plant-shoot and its effort to survive the wind shows characteristics like strength, flexibility, independence, patience and fighting spirit.

The young plant is trying to survive against the wind and to keep itself rooted. In order to do so, it needs flexibility, strength and patience. Hence Swati exhibits characteristics like strength, flexibility, fighting spirit, patience and independence. Survival of a plant through storms or problems means the plant is going to grow to its fullest potential, over a longer period of time. Hence Swati exhibits characteristics of growing at slow but steady pace; fighting and surviving the obstacles on the way.

A coral is also taken as a symbol of Swati, according to some beliefs of Vedic astrology. Coral is known as a plant which grows by itself with the help of some micro-organisms and it does not need any external factors for its growth and survival. This symbol exhibits characteristics like self-dependence, hard work and patience; and all these characteristics are exhibited by Swati.

Hence Swati is considered as a nakshatra which promotes and supports characteristics like self- dependence, delicacy, flexibility, patience and strength. Therefore, natives under strong influence of Swati are capable of building themselves from nothing, even when there is no outside support available.

Though there are other nakshatras which show characteristics like independence and fighting spirit like Ashwini, Swati is unique in its own way. Ashwini is independent but it doesn't care whether or not it survives. It means Ashwini natives may use independence as their goal and they may not bother about what they achieve through such independence.

On the other hand, Swati promotes characteristics like independence, self-dependence, patience, the ability to survive and the ability to achieve. It means natives under strong influence of Swati may work for survival and growth; and independence may be among one of the tools they use to achieve their goals. In other words, Ashwini fulfills its wish when it achieves independence whereas Swati fulfills its wish while being independent.

Hence independence is the final destination for Ashwini whereas it is a method of reaching the final destination for Swati. Looking at it from another angle, Ashwini is happy in being independent and making efforts, not caring about results in most cases. On the other hand, Swati ensures that it achieves results through characteristics like independence, patience, flexibility and strength. It means Swati may be better in comparison to Ashwini, when it comes to deliver results, especially materialistic results.

Vedic astrology assigns god Vaayu, the god of wind, as the ruling deity of Swati. As already seen in the discussion related to the symbol of Swati, Vaayu or wind has a lot to do with this nakshatra. Vaayu is one of the five main gods residing in Swarg Loka (Heaven). He is in charge of air element which is one of the five main elements known as earth, water, fire, air and ether. Since Vaayu is the ruling deity of Swati; many characteristics of Vaayu like strength, flexibility, intellect, indecisiveness and adaptability are relayed through this nakshatra.

As a result, natives under strong influence of Swati may be strong, flexible and intellectual. At the same time, they may be good at the art of socializing and accommodating; since they may be flexible and adaptive. Air has no shape and it can fit into any space and in any shape. Hence Swati natives may be able to fit into a number of different situations and they may able to handle a number of different types of people.

Goddess Saraswati is considered as the second ruling deity of Swati. Saraswati is the goddess of knowledge, learning, music, voice and speech. All these characteristics of goddess Saraswati are exhibited through Swati. Vedic astrology assigns Rahu as the planetary ruler of Swati. Rahu is generally known as a planet of mysteries but it releases its characteristics like diplomacy, social bonding, ability as well as willingness to learn and other likewise characteristics through Swati.

Goddess Saraswati is also considered as the ruling deity of Rahu. Therefore, those characteristics of Rahu which are in harmony with the characteristics of goddess Saraswati are more likely to be relayed through Swati, as this nakshatra is under the combined influence of goddess Saraswati and Rahu.

Due to these characteristics, natives under strong influence of Swati may do well in creative fields as well as in fields which deal with some type of learning or teaching. When supported by overall horoscope, strong influence of Swati may produce some of the best singers, dancers and musicians; among other creative artists.

All four quarters of Swati fall in Libra which is an air sign ruled by Venus. Venus is known as a social, diplomatic and indulgent planet. It is important to note that the main ruling deity of Swati is Vaayu who is the ruler of the air element. The planetary ruler of Swati is Rahu which is also considered as an airy planet. All quarters of Swati fall in Libra which again is an air sign.

Hence Swati has a strong connection with air element. Accordingly, it is very likely to exhibit characteristics which are airy in nature. For example, natives under strong influence of Swati may take long in order to make decisions. This is primarily due to strong airy nature of Swati, as air is associated with indecisiveness and instability.

Therefore, Swati needs support from fire element to make decisions and then execute them. At the same time, it needs support from earth element in order to stick to its actions. This is because fire element is good at initiating things and converting thoughts into actions, but it generally doesn't care much about taking such actions through to the end.

Hence natives under strong influence of Swati should have strong planets which represent initiative, like Sun and Mars. At the same time, they should also have strong planets which represent stability, like Saturn. Sun and Mars may help Swati natives make quick decisions and then convert them to actions. Saturn may help Swati natives stick to such actions and take them through to the end. In an extreme case when four or five planets are placed in Swati in a relevant house of a horoscope and Sun as well as Mars is weak; the native may not achieve much. Such native may think a lot and he may not be able to convert his thoughts into actions.

Swati natives may have tendencies to show off. This is because Rahu and Venus have strong influence over Swati and both these planets are known as indulgent ones. Rahu is especially known for acts of showing off. The combined influence of Venus and Rahu makes Swati an indulgent nakshatra. Accordingly, natives under strong influence of Swati may be seen pursuing and indulging in many types of materialistic pursuits.

Whether such material pursuits are within limits or beyond limits depends on which planets occupy Swati in a horoscope. Likewise, whether such material pursuits are moral or immoral depends on the benefic or malefic nature of planets placed in Swati. When working strongly without any planetary influences which means when rising in the ascendant without any planets placed in it; Swati may make the native somewhat more indulgent but not immoral.

However, if it is occupied by planets like Mars, Venus, Rahu or Ketu, Swati may become over indulgent. If such planets are malefic in nature; Swati may become over indulgent as well as immoral. In such cases, natural characteristics of Swati may be corrupted and it may work in ways; which may not do justice to the general image of this nakshatra.

On the other hand, placement of Saturn in Swati may help it behave in balanced and moral ways; provided Saturn is benefic in the horoscope under consideration. Placement of Moon in Swati may make it somewhat more indulgent but not immoral; provided Moon is benefic in the horoscope under consideration. Placement of Jupiter or Mercury may swing this nakshatra either way; depending on the overall horoscope of the native under consideration. Since Sun gets debilitated in Libra, it may not do much to affect the characteristics of Swati, when placed in it.

Swati natives may have tendency to wait for long periods of time in order to achieve desired results. When their overall horoscopes are supportive, this characteristic may prove beneficial, helping these natives achieve a lot through patience. However, if their overall horoscopes are not supportive, this characteristic of Swati may become a negative one. Such Swati natives may keep waiting for desired results, even when there may be no reasonable possibility of materialization of such results.

Taking an example, if Moon is placed in the first house of a horoscope in Swati along with malefic Ketu, forming Grahan Yoga; and Sun, Jupiter, Mercury and Mars are weak or afflicted in the horoscope; the native may face problems. Such native may not be able to decide how much to wait and when to move on. As a result, he may keep waiting for certain results or for some people; even when there may be no realistic hopes of achieving them. This may end up creating problems for the native.

Looking at a different probability, if a benefic combination of Moon and Mars forms Chandra Mangal Yoga in the first house of a horoscope with Moon in Swati; and Saturn as well as Sun are strong in the horoscope, the results may change. The native in this case may know when to wait and when to move on, and he may not face problems due to waiting too long.

When Swati is not supported by suitable planetary energies in a horoscope, natives under its strong influence may have inability to make decisions in time. They may also have inability to convert their ideas to practical work or execution, though their ideas may be very good and capable of producing favourable results if executed in time.

Therefore, one of the biggest challenges for natives under strong influence of Swati may be that they need to learn to make decisions in time and then execute such decisions in time. By doing so, these natives may achieve a lot in their lives and they may make best use of energies of Swati.

Strong influence of Swati may bless the natives with very good and innovative ideas; and all they need to do is to execute such ideas. Therefore, the difference between successful and unsuccessful Swati natives may very well be the ability or inability to make decisions and then execute such decisions. In most cases, such ability is rendered by suitable benefic planets in a horoscope; as Swati on its own may not be able to make and execute decisions in time, in many cases.

Swati natives may be beautiful and attractive due to influence of Venus; if this nakshatra rises in the ascendant. Swati natives may be good at the art of diplomacy as diplomacy is primarily an airy characteristic. Diplomacy needs flexibility and air is known to be very flexible. Apart from that, both Rahu and Venus are known as diplomatic planets. Accordingly, their influences on Swati make it exhibit characteristics like diplomacy and flexibility.

Swati natives may be good at social skills. Hence they may be found at social get-togethers and parties; socializing with different types of people. Swati natives may be very much inclined to social networking. In the present times, the concept of social networking websites like Facebook is growing, primarily because of influence of Swati. Both Venus and Rahu love to socialize; where Rahu rules internet and websites. It means Swati natives may benefit from professions related to internet, websites and social networking.

Looking at the bigger picture, Swati has a great deal of contribution in shaping up today's world and society. This is because people are choosing to practice social networking more and more through internet, websites and applications. All this may be seen as strong influence of Swati on people as well as on society as whole. Hence Swati may be considered as a nakshatra which makes social bonds and networking happen, especially through internet, phones and other such concepts.

Therefore, a number of people having big social networks are likely to be under strong influence of Swati. Swati natives may be good at making adjustments in most situations due to their flexible natures. As a result, they may be better at making and keeping their social relationships. It should be noted that in present times; Swati promotes social networking more through media like internet, mobile phones, websites and applications. This is because Rahu has strong influence on the current phase of time. Since Rahu prefers virtual concepts more than physical concepts, social networking is being promoted through virtual platforms like internet.

Looking at it from another angle, Rahu rules the Maya or Illusion element of nature. Everything happening over internet is more like illusion than the real thing. This is why more and more virtual phenomena like virtual assistance, virtual teaching, virtual gaming experience and virtual sex are taking place.

When it comes to pure influence of Venus; it likes the real thing and it doesn't believe much in virtual thing. It means a native under strong influence of pure Venus is more likely to believe in social networking through parties, social gatherings, get-togethers and other such concepts, instead of going for options like internet and other such media.

Even when it comes to relationships; Venus believes in physical touch and it doesn't believe much in doing things virtually. Hence a native under strong influence of Venus and weak influence of Rahu may still believe in traditional type of dating where lovers meet, talk and enjoy. One such native may not be much fond of getting in touch with his lover through text messages and applications of various types.

Since Swati is ruled by Rahu and it is influenced by Venus; these energies operate through a common platform. Hence Venus adds the need to socialize and Rahu adds the need to virtualize. As a result, natives under strong influence of Swati may be skilled at socializing, especially through virtual platforms like internet. It should be noted that this characteristic may change in some horoscopes, depending on placements of various planets in Swati.

Swati natives are generally patient. They can make investments and wait for long periods of times for those investments to mature and bring fruits. These investments may be financial, emotional, professional or other types of investments, depending on placements of various planets in Swati; and on overall horoscopes of these natives.

Due to the characteristic of patience exhibited by Swati, Saturn gains maximum strength in Swati. It means Saturn achieves its point of maximum exaltation in Swati; within the sign of Libra. This is because Saturn loves nothing more than patience and discipline; and Swati is loaded with patience. Therefore, it is in Swati where Saturn may do its best work, though such work may be positive or negative; depending on functional nature of Saturn in the horoscope under consideration.

Looking at an interesting fact; Saturn is exalted in its sign of placement as well as navamsha; when it is placed in Libra navamsha of Chitra. However, it may still be stronger and it may perform better when it is placed in Capricorn or Aquarius navamsha of Swati. This is because Chitra is an aggressive nakshatra whereas Swati is a patient nakshatra. Hence Saturn may feel more comfortable in Swati than in Chitra. When assessing the strength of a planet; its comfort in a sign, nakshatra as well as navamsha should be duly checked.

Moving on, Sun is known as the planet of quick decision and execution. Sun is also considered as the peak of individualism among navagraha. On the contrary, Libra is a sign which strongly promotes the concept of society, leaving little space for individualism. It means the general characteristics of Sun are in opposition to those of Libra, in this particular aspect.

Sun wishes to focus on the self, whereas Libra wants to focus on society and relationships. Since there is an obvious clash between priorities, the combination of Sun and Libra doesn't work well on its own. As a result, Sun gets debilitated in Libra and within Libra also, it feels choked in Swati.

Looking at an interesting fact; Sun is debilitated in its sign of placement as well as navamsha; when it is placed in Libra navamsha of Chitra. However, it may still be weaker and it may perform worse when it is placed in Aquarius navamsha of Swati. This is because Chitra is an aggressive nakshatra rules by Mars and Sun is very comfortable in this nakshatra. On the other hand, Swati is a patient, flexible and social nakshatra. Hence Sun may feel much discomfort in Swati. Apart from that, Sun may feel choked when placed in Aquarius. As the combined result of these factors; Sun may perform worse in Aquarius navamsha of Swati than in Libra navamsha of Chitra.

Though Swati exhibits a number of characteristics, different natives may embrace different characteristics, depending on placements of various planets in this nakshatra, as well as on their overall horoscopes. Looking at planets; Moon, Venus, Mars, Mercury, Saturn and Rahu may do well in Swati. Jupiter may perform well in this nakshatra, if the overall horoscope is supportive. Sun and Ketu are generally not suited for energy of Swati. Placements of malefic planets in Swati can cause various types of problems for the native, depending on his overall horoscope.

Let's look at performances of various planets in various navamshas of Swati. Starting with Sagittarius navamsha; Venus, Rahu and Saturn may perform well or very well here whereas Mercury may perform well but not very well here. Mercury is not as strong in Libra as Venus and Saturn; and it is not as good in Swati as Rahu.

Moon, Jupiter and Mars may perform on average or above average in this navamsha; depending on the overall horoscope. Ketu may perform on average in this navamsha. Sun may perform below average here and if the overall horoscope is supportive; it may perform on average here. Among navagraha; Venus may be the strongest in this navamsha whereas Sun may be the weakest.

Looking at Capricorn navamsha; Venus, Saturn, Mercury and Rahu may perform well or very well here; since they are all strong in Libra as well as Capricorn. Moon may perform above average in this navamsha; since it is very comfortable in Swati and it has decent strength in Libra as well as Capricorn.

Mars may perform well in this navamsha whereas Jupiter may perform poorly here. Mars is exalted in Capricorn whereas Jupiter is debilitated in this sign. Sun may perform below average or poorly in this navamsha whereas Ketu may perform on average in this navamsha. Among navagraha; Saturn may be the strongest in this navamsha whereas Sun may be the weakest in this navamsha.

Moving on to Aquarius navamsha; Venus, Saturn, Rahu and Mercury may perform well or very well here; since they are all strong in Libra as well as Aquarius. Moon may perform on average or below average in this navamsha; since it is not comfortable in Aquarius.

Mars may perform on average or below average here and Jupiter may also do the same; since both of them are not strong in Libra as well as Aquarius. Ketu may perform on average here. Sun may perform poorly or very poorly in this navamsha; since it is uncomfortable in Libra, Swati and Aquarius. Among all 108 navamshas of 27 nakshatras; Sun may deliver its worst performance in this navamsha. Among navagraha; Saturn may be the strongest in this navamsha whereas Sun may be the weakest.

Considering Pisces navamsha; Venus may perform very well here whereas Saturn may perform well or very well in this navamsha; depending on the overall horoscope. Venus is exalted in Pisces whereas Saturn is not strong in this sign. Mercury and Rahu may perform well or above average in this navamsha; since both of them are debilitated in Pisces.

Moon may perform well in this navamsha; since it is strong in Pisces and it has fair strength in Libra. Jupiter may perform above average here; since it is strong in Pisces but not strong in Libra. Mars may perform on average or below average here whereas Ketu may perform above average or well in this navamsha. Ketu is exalted in Pisces. Sun may perform below average or poorly in this navamsha. Among navagraha; Venus may be the strongest in this navamsha whereas Sun may be the weakest.

Looking at professions, natives under strong influence of Swati may achieve success as singers, musicians, actors, writers, poets, dancers, designers, fashion models, architects, politicians, administrative officers, diplomats, revenue officers; professionals dealing in internet industry, website industry, social media industry, telecom industry, event management industry, matrimonial services, match making industry, dating platforms, hotel industry, airline industry, tour and travel industry, liquor industry, tobacco industry, movie industry, television industry, fashion industry; all industries coming under entertainment, luxury and arts; ecommerce industry, logistics industry, international trades; astrologers, consultants, marriage counselors, engineers, doctors, lawyers and many other types of professionals; depending on their overall horoscopes.

Let's look at some other facts associated with this nakshatra. Swati is considered as a passive and movable nakshatra. It is considered as a female nakshatra. Vedic astrology assigns Butcher Varna and fire element to Swati. The Gana assigned to Swati is Deva and the Guna assigned to it is Rajasic. It is a level nakshatra and its Yoni or animal symbol is Buffalo.

Vishakha

Vishakha is 16th among 27 nakshatras. The first three quarters of Vishakha fall in Libra whereas the last quarter of this nakshatra falls in Scorpio.

The meanings of the word Vishakha are translated in Vedic astrology as two-branched, divided or having more than one branch. Accordingly, it is believed that natives under strong influence of Vishakha may face such situations many times in their lives where they have to choose between two or more paths or options. The success or failure of Vishakha natives may depend on whether they choose right path or wrong.

The characteristic of having to choose among different options is one of most prominent characteristics of Vishakha. The main symbol of Vishakha is a decorated gateway, as per Vedic astrology. This gateway is like the ones which are used as welcome gates during Indian marriage ceremonies and some other types of ceremonies.

Such gates are mostly associated with outward display of some kind of achievement or objective that someone has reached. After such achievement, the native may want to celebrate and show off. Accordingly, Vishakha exhibits characteristics like promoting the outward display of achievements, show off and show biz. Hence Vishakha natives may be natural show offs. These natives may simply love to show their proud possessions and achievements to the world.

A traditional marriage ceremony in India is a show of wealth, status and position of a family. Through this ceremony, a family shows off its achievements and tries to impress society. A decorated gate is an important part of this theme of showing off since people enter the venue through this gate. It means bigger the status of a family is, bigger is the show-off and more decorated is the gateway.

Since marriage is the beginning of a new relationship, Vishakha promotes new beginnings of various types. Decorated gateways are also used for other ceremonies like the ones which are arranged when people have achieved success, recognition or some important milestones in their lives. All these ceremonies as well as decorated gates display money, resources, power, possessions and beauty. Hence Vishakha exhibits all these characteristics.

Since the urge to achieve and the urge to celebrate and show off after achievements is strong in present times; Vishakha becomes an important nakshatra in these times. Vishakha natives are ambitious and they wish to achieve a lot. Once they have achieved, Vishakha natives may want to show such achievements off to the world, through parties and celebrations.

As Vishakha is directly associated with achievements, celebrations and acts of show off, natives under its strong influence may often be found dealing in professions which feature these characteristics. It means Vishakha natives may achieve success in movie industry, television industry, fashion industry and other such professions. A number of celebrities in glamour world are under strong influence of Vishakha.

Vedic astrology assigns two ruling deities to Vishakha. These two deities are known as god Indra, the ruler of heaven and god Agni, the ruler of Fire. Hence, Vishakha exhibits a number of characteristics which are displayed by its ruling deities. Let's look at some characteristics displayed by Indra and Agni.

According to Vedic mythology, Indra is considered as the ruler of heaven as well as the ruler of all gods including Agni. Vedic mythology portrays Indra as the one who is very much goal oriented. Indra is many times scared of losing his throne to someone else and he often tries to save his throne. In attempts to keep his throne intact, he commits various types of immoral deeds from time to time, according to Vedic mythology.

For example, Indra once tried to kill the pregnant wife of demon Hiranyakshipu in order to stop him from worshipping Lord Brahma. The demon was worshipping the Lord in order to get blessed with great powers. Indra feared that HiranyaKshipu would gain powers, attack heaven and remove him from his throne. Therefore, in order to save his throne, he tried to disturb the worship of Hiranyakshipu through every possible way.

When he did not succeed by any means, he kidnapped pregnant wife of Hiranyakshipu and took her to the place where the demon was worshipping. Indra threatened the demon that if he did not stop the worship, he would kill demon's pregnant wife along with his future child. It was only after the intervention of divine sage Naarad that Indra could be stopped from killing pregnant wife of Hiranyakshipu.

From the above example, it can be seen that Indra is a very goal oriented deity and he can go to any lengths to achieve his goals. Indra can also engage in any karma whether good or bad, in order to achieve his goals. This goal oriented characteristic of Indra is relayed through Vishakha. Accordingly, natives under strong influence of Vishakha may be fixated on their goals. Hence such Vishakha natives may be in danger of engaging in bad karmas or immoral deeds in order to achieve their goals.

Indra is also known for his deep interests in drinking, women and enjoying other pleasures. All these characteristics of Indra are also relayed through Vishakha. As a result, Vishakha natives are likely to be fond of materialistic pleasures of all types. These characteristics are promoted by Libra part of Vishakha whereas they may be relatively subdued in Scorpio part of this nakshatra.

The expression of these characteristics may vary in quality as well as in quantity; depending on planets which occupy Vishakha, as well as on the overall horoscope of the native under consideration. For example, if Mars is placed in the first house of a horoscope in Libra in Vishakha, the native may indulge in company of women and he may also be fond of liquor, unless there are corrective planets in the horoscope.

However, if Rahu is placed in the first house of a horoscope in Libra in Vishakha, the native may develop taste for various types of drugs; apart from consuming alcohol. Such native may also be fond of women and he may love engaging in sexual pleasures of various types.

Looking at another probability, If Venus forms Malavya Yoga in the first house of a horoscope in Libra in Vishakha, the native may be interested in women and alcohol, but he may be even more interested in money, wealth, houses, cars and other pursuits of luxury. Formation of this type of Malavya Yoga in the horoscope of a female native may bless her with luring beauty as well as with success in professions falling under the field of glamour.

Luring beauty means such female native may be good at provoking the senses of viewers; and that too without much effort. Female natives under strong influence of this type of Malavya Yoga may not be the most beautiful ones, as placements of Venus in some other nakshatras can bless them with even more beauty. However, such female natives may certainly be among the most desirable types of females.

Vishakha is all about desires and their fulfillments. Since a female is a general signifier of Venus, formation of Malavya Yoga in the first house in Libra in Vishakha can make a female native most desirable.

Drawing a comparison, female natives under strong influence of Malavya Yoga in the first house in Swati may inspire more appreciation than desire; by virtue of their beauty. On the other hand, female natives with such Malavya Yoga in Vishakha may inspire more desire than appreciation; by virtue of their beauty. Hence you may love and appreciate the Swati type female but you may desire Vishakha type female.

Moving on, if exalted Saturn forms Shasha Yoga in the first house of a horoscope in Libra in Vishakha, all such tendencies may be put under check. The native in this case may enjoy alcohol and women also; but only occasionally. Such native under strong influence of Shasha Yoga in Vishakha may be much more focused on professional success and raising wealth, than engaging himself in various types of pleasures at the cost of professional success and health.

Placement of Moon in the first house in Libra in Vishakha in the horoscope of a male native may incline him towards various types of pleasures, including the company of females.

However, such native may not go to extremes in most cases. The same placement of Moon in Vishakha in the horoscope of a female native may bend her more towards professional success and raising wealth; than engaging in bodily pleasures.

Coming back to ruling deities of Vishakha, Agni rules fire element according to Vedic mythology and he is portrayed as the one with good character. The influence of Agni on Vishakha brings sufficient energy to this nakshatra, which can help natives under its influence achieve their goals.

A relevant incident is quoted in Vedic mythology where a demon prayed to god Agni to protect him. After receiving assurance from Agni, he started worshipping lord Brahma for gaining powers. Indra, seeing it as threat to his power came to kill the demon. However, Agni who had promised the demon to protect him, came in the way and fought Indra; preventing him from killing the demon. It should be noted that Agni fought with Indra in order to do what was right, despite the fact that Indra was his king.

This incident is closely related to the divided personality of Vishakha. It means the influence of Agni on Vishakha brings positive characteristics of Agni and influence of Indra on this nakshatra adds his questionable characteristics to Vishakha. This further means that natives under strong influence of Vishakha may witness constant battle inside them, as if two sides of their personalities are fighting with each other.

Whenever an opportunity presents itself, the influence of Indra may encourage converting such opportunity at any cost. On the other hand, the influence of Agni may encourage assessing the cost first and then deciding whether to proceed or not. It means the first side wants to achieve success at any cost whereas the second side likes to quit; if such success is achieved through immoral ways.

Hence the biggest task of a native under strong influence of Vishakha may be to decide which side he wants to embrace, along with all its consequences. In a horoscope, placements of various benefic or malefic planets in Vishakha may indicate which one of these sides the native is more likely to embrace.

Vedic astrology assigns Jupiter as the ruling planet of Vishakha. A number of characteristics of Jupiter find expression through Vishakha. It is interesting to note that many of these characteristics may be used negatively due to strong influence of Indra on Vishakha. For example, Jupiter's ability and optimism for achieving goals may be used negatively through Vishakha as the goals set by Vishakha may not be in tune with universal wellbeing, in many cases.

The first three quarters of Vishakha fall in Libra ruled by Venus and the last quarter falls in Scorpio ruled by Mars. The Libra part of Vishakha comes under the influence of planets with opposite natures just as it comes under the influence of deities with different natures. Jupiter and Venus are different in many of their characteristics and they are opposite in some of their characteristics.

A double set of opposite influences makes Vishakha a hard to balance nakshatra. This is probably the reason why the name of this nakshatra has been chosen Vishakha since it is divided between conflicting ruling deities as well as between conflicting planets. It can be seen that Indra's love for drinking, women, pomp, power and show is more in tune with Venus than Jupiter. Hence the Indra side of Vishakha is likely to be the dominant side, in Libra part of this nakshatra.

Accordingly, natives under strong influence of Libra part of Vishakha may get fixated on their goals. These natives may not care much whether the paths they are choosing to reach these goals are right or wrong. As a result, these natives may have tendency to choose wrong paths at many points in their lives. For such Vishakha natives, only the goals may be important and the means may not be. Vishakha is a nakshatra of desire and the desire element may exhibit fully in Libra part of this nakshatra.

Vishakha natives may be fond of alcohol, sex and other pleasures of senses. They may also be strong followers of pomp and extravagance. To fulfill these desires, they may need a lot of money and resources. Quite often, earning such amounts of money through right paths may be difficult. Hence natives under strong influence of Vishakha may end up following wrong paths in their lives.

This is because getting what they want may be of prime importance to them and how they get it may not be much important. Vishakha natives may be easily charmed by materialistic pleasures and they may have strong urges to experience them. Vishakha natives may have strong fires of desires burning inside them. No matter how much they may try to satisfy their desires, they may end up wanting more in most cases.

As a result, strong influence of Vishakha can make the natives reach for excesses in the fields like alcohol, sex and other physical pleasures. Vishakha natives may not bother much about moral and ethical codes of society. They may be focused at reaching their goals which may many times not be in tune with moral and ethical codes of society.

Vishakha may give strong will power to achieve goals. It may also bless the natives with love for life and the ability to celebrate life. However, these positive characteristics may need a check on them as they may easily cross their limits and change into negative ones. The key element for Vishakha is the kind of path it chooses, depending on how its energy is channelized.

If the energy of Vishakha is used by suitable benefic planets; it may follow the right path and it may bless the native with a number of good results. However, if the energy of Vishakha is used by opportunistic or malefic planets; the native may end up losing more than he gains. It means such native may engage in various types of immoral and bad karmas, inviting a number of problems for near and far future.

Vishakha natives may do well or very well in professions; depending on their overall horoscopes. Placements of suitable benefic planets in Vishakha may bless a native with millions or billions through profession, provided his overall horoscope is supportive. Such natives may have very good chances of achieving success in professional spheres which deal with glamour, entertainment, luxuries, relaxation, pleasure of senses, beauty and other likewise fields. Hence some Vishakha natives may achieve success as movie stars whereas some others may succeed in hotel industry. Some of these natives may engage in airline industry, some may engage in casino industry and some others may achieve success through liquor industry.

The sphere of personal life and relationships may not do well in case of these natives. Vishakha natives may be good at getting into relationships. Hence they may make friends, lovers and associates quickly. However, they may not be good at maintaining such relationships. Hence people may come in and go out of their lives; often leaving voids which may be filled by other people; and this trend may continue almost throughout their lives.

The major reason for this trend may be that Vishakha natives may give much more priority to their professional goals and materialistic desires; compared to people. Hence when a situation arises where one such native may have to choose between an opportunity for professional growth and someone close to him or someone he loves; such native may often choose the former.

Though one such native may still care for his loved one; he may care more for his goals. Hence he may want his loved ones to follow him or walk with him on any path he chooses. Since such paths may often be troublesome ones; his loved ones may choose not to walk on them. Instead they may advise/warn him to stay away from such paths. This may leave one such native with a choice to make between such path and one such loved one.

Many times, the native may choose the path over such loved one, since materialistic success and goals may be on the top of his list of priorities. Hence he may often sacrifice people closer to him; though he may not wish to. It means what he may really want is for such people to walk along with him on the paths chosen by him. Failing to convince them to do so; he may walk alone on such paths.

For this reason, Vishakha natives may witness people coming in and going out of their lives. Only those people may stay longer with them; who may have similar priorities; which means who may be willing to walk on any path to achieve what they want. Due to this characteristic; Vishakha natives may want people around them to understand them whereas they may not be willing to do the same. Hence they may expect many compromises from people close to them and in return; they may not be willing to make many compromises or any compromises.

This attitude may especially prove troublesome for relationships like marriage and love affair; since their partners may often feel ignored due to fixation of these natives on materialistic goals. The same fixation may often bless them with good or very good amount of professional success and money; though it may cost them dearly in the sphere of relationships.

This tendency may be higher in Libra part of Vishakha, compared to Scorpio part of this nakshatra. Hence natives under strong influence of Scorpio part of Vishakha may not suffer that much in the sphere of relationships; since they may often make compromises for the people who matter to them. Such Vishakha natives may care a lot for their goals but they may also care a lot for people close to them.

Hence they may at times sacrifice the opportunities for materialistic growth, for their loved ones. At other times, they may be able to convince such loved ones to walk along with them on the paths chosen by them. This way, they may do better in the sphere of relationships; than those under strong influence of Libra part of Vishakha. The Indra part of Vishakha may dominate in Libra whereas the Agni part of Vishakha may dominate or put a strong fight in Scorpio.

Though Vishakha displays a number of characteristics, different natives may embrace different characteristics, depending on placements of various planets in this nakshatra, as well as on their overall horoscopes. Looking at planets; Moon, Venus, Mercury, Rahu and Saturn may perform better in Libra part of Vishakha. Sun, Mars, Jupiter and Ketu may perform better in Scorpio part of Vishakha.

Vishakha is a difficult to handle nakshatra. Hence placements of malefic planets in Vishakha may cause a number of problems for the native; depending on his overall horoscope. Vishakha is prone to pay more than it achieves, in the long run. It means many Vishakha natives may witness considerable gains in the short run, but they may end up suffering more, in the long run. Therefore, natives under its strong influence should keep their desires in check; so that they don't go against the universal theme.

Let's look at performances of various planets in various navamshas of Vishakha. Starting with Aries navamsha; Venus may do very well in this navamsha whereas Mercury, Rahu and Saturn may do well but not very well in this navamsha. Saturn is exalted in Libra but it is debilitated in Aries. Mars may perform above average or well in this navamsha; since it has decent strength in Libra, it is strong in Aries and it is very comfortable in Vishakha.

Jupiter may perform above average or well in this navamsha; since it rules Vishakha and it is strong in Aries. Moon may perform above average here; since it may do well in Libra as well as Aries but it is not strong in any one of them. Ketu may perform above average in this navamsha. Sun may perform on average or above average here; since it is exalted in Aries and very comfortable in Vishakha; but debilitated in Libra. Within the sign of Libra; Sun may be the least weak in this navamsha. Among navagraha; Venus may be the strongest in this navamsha. No planet may be significantly weak in this navamsha and no planet may perform below average or poorly here.

Looking at Taurus navamsha; Venus, Saturn, Mercury and Rahu may perform very well here; since they are all strong in Libra as well as Taurus. Moon may perform well in this navamsha; since it has fair strength in Libra and it is exalted in Taurus. Jupiter may perform on average or above average but not well here; since it is not strong in Libra as well as Taurus.

Mars may perform on average or above average here; since it is very comfortable in Vishakha but it is not strong in Libra as well as Taurus. Ketu may perform below average here; since it is not strong in Libra and it is debilitated in

Taurus. Sun may perform below average or poorly here; since it is not strong in Taurus and it is debilitated in Libra; though it is very comfortable in Vishakha. Among navagraha; Venus and Saturn may be the strongest in this navamsha whereas Sun may be the weakest.

Moving on to Gemini navamsha; Venus, Saturn, Mercury and Rahu may perform well or very well here; since they are all strong in Libra as well as Gemini. Moon may perform on average in this navamsha; since it is not strong in Libra as well as Gemini. Jupiter may also perform on average here; for the same reasons as Moon.

Mars may perform on average or above average in this navamsha; since it is very comfortable in Vishakha but it is not strong in Libra as well as Gemini. Ketu may perform below average here; since it is not strong in Libra and it is weak in Gemini. Sun may perform poorly in this navamsha; since it is debilitated in Libra and not strong in Gemini. Among navagraha; Venus and Saturn may be the strongest in this navamsha whereas Sun may be the weakest.

Considering Cancer navamsha; Jupiter and Ketu may perform well or very well here. Jupiter is strong in Scorpio and exalted in Cancer whereas Ketu has decent strength in Cancer and it is exalted in Scorpio. Mars may perform well but not very well here; since it is strong in Scorpio but debilitated in Cancer. Sun may perform on average or above average here; since it has good strength in Scorpio and it is very comfortable in Vishakha, but it is weak in Cancer.

Venus may perform above average in this navamsha; since it is not strong in Scorpio as well as Cancer. Mercury and Saturn may perform on average here; since none of them is strong in Scorpio as well as Cancer. Moon may perform below average in this navamsha; since it is debilitated in Scorpio but it is strong in Cancer. Rahu may perform poorly here; since it is debilitated in Scorpio and not strong in Cancer. Among navagraha; Ketu may be the strongest in this navamsha whereas Rahu may be the weakest.

Looking at professions, natives under strong influence of Vishakha may achieve success as models, actors, singers, musicians, dancers, writers, sportsmen, TV and radio artists, bartenders, pub owners and other professionals dealing in liquor industry; professionals working in sex industry like prostitutes, gigolos, porn artists, porn directors; drug dealers, arms dealers, gangsters, liquor smugglers, professionals dealing in sex rackets, militants, politicians, government officers, defense professionals, astrologers, psychics, healers, consultants, scientists, engineers, professionals dealing in movie industry, fashion industry, television industry, music industry, hotel industry, airline industry, casinos, tour and travel industry, apparel industry, tobacco industry and many other types of professionals, depending on their overall horoscopes.

Let's look at some other facts associated with this nakshatra. Vishakha is considered as an active and mixed nakshatra. It is considered as a female nakshatra. Vedic astrology assigns Shudra Varna and fire element to Vishakha. The Gana assigned to Vishakha is Rakshasa and the Guna assigned to it is Sattwic. It is a downward nakshatra and its Yoni or animal symbol is Tiger.

Anuradha

Anuradha is 17th among 27 nakshatras. All four quarters of Anuradha fall in Scorpio. The word Anuradha literally translates into 'another Radha'. Prevalent beliefs of Vedic astrology relate the meaning of this word to success and good luck.

Radha was Lord Krishna's lover and their relationship had significant amounts of friendship and understanding among other attributes. To be the love of Lord Krishna is considered as great luck and success. The love of Radha for Lord Krishna was intense and soft at the same time. It means her love was not filled with possession and it was liberating type. Hence characteristics like friendship, understanding, intensity, liberty, luck and success are added to Anuradha through its name. Due to these characteristics, natives under strong influence of Anuradha may be friendly, caring, liberal, intense and understanding.

The main symbol of Anuradha is a staff carried by powerful sages according to Vedic mythology. These staffs used to be very powerful. They were used by sages for protection and to punish the ones who deserved punishments. It means staffs were used by them to keep things around them in balance. The sages almost never used their staffs for selfish motives. They used their staffs only when there was need for them to be used, which means they used them wisely.

Hence the symbol of staff associates Anuradha with power, protection and wisdom. Accordingly, these characteristics are relayed through Anuradha, combining with the characteristics mentioned earlier. An alternate symbol of Lotus is also assigned to Anuradha. Lotus is considered as a very auspicious flower in Vedic mythology. It is considered as the Aasana or seat of goddess Saraswati, the goddess of learning and knowledge.

A lotus is special in the way that it grows in mud and it stays in mud, but it doesn't get affected by it. This means despite growing in mud; lotus keeps itself clean and pure. A lotus conveys that in the deepest sense, purity is not dependent on circumstances outside, it comes from within. A Lotus also shows that life may take beautiful forms, even by using resources like mud.

It means spiritual advancement or goodness may be achieved, even when all around you is bad. It also means that a wise person can make constructive use of even the negative people or circumstances around him. He may do so by learning how not to be like them and why not to do what they are doing. For these reasons, Lotus is considered as an inspiration for natives who wish to achieve spiritual growth or who wish to make themselves better, even when circumstances may be adverse. Therefore, Anuradha is also associated with characteristics like learning, auspiciousness, enlightenment, wisdom and the ability to remain unaffected by circumstances.

Vedic astrology assigns Mitra, one of the twelve Adityas (Solar deities) as the ruling deity of Anuradha. Accordingly, many characteristics of Mitra are relayed through Anuradha. The word Mitra translates into Friend. Hence the characteristics like friendliness, cordiality, helpfulness and working in harmony with others to achieve success are associated with Mitra. All these characteristics find expression through Anuradha. Mitra promotes friendship on all levels and stages of life. Hence Anuradha may be seen as a nakshatra which promotes friendship and universal brotherhood.

As a result, Anuradha natives may be seen making many friends throughout their lives. Such natives may achieve success with the help of these friends and as results of group work. It should be noted that while making friends, Anuradha may not discriminate based on age, race, colour, gender, financial status and all other such attributes. For this reason, natives under strong influence of Anuradha may have large networks of friends, belonging to all walks of life.

An adult male native having a number of friends including aged people, females, children or young ones; natives belonging to different religions, races, colors and beliefs; may very well be an Anuradha native. It should however be noted that Anuradha works on the basis of sharing and it generally doesn't promote unconditional friendship. It means an Anuradha native may prove one of your best friends if you are looking for help, support and understanding; and you are willing to offer the same when he is in need.

However, if you are looking for a friend who you only wish to gain from and offer little in return; an Anuradha native may not fit this choice. Anuradha natives are sharp and wise enough to separate genuine friends from selfish ones. Hence they may not stay for long with you, if they find out that you are in friendship, only for your gains. It means friendship offered by Anuradha comes with expectation for return.

Anuradha natives may not be greedy and all they may want are relationships which work on the basis of mutual benefits. Here also, they may not count favours. It means Anuradha natives may not want their friends to do favours for them, in return for each favour these natives do for such friends.

All these natives may be looking for is that their friends are there when they need them. Therefore, an Anuradha native may give you ten times more favours than you do and he may still consider you a good friend; if you are there when he needs you. Hence natives under strong influence of Anuradha may not be selfish or too calculative when it comes to friendship.

However, they may want friendship which is mutual and they may not believe in one way friendship. Compared to this, natives under strong influence of Revati may continue to be your friends, even if you often don't show up when they need you. The friendship or love of Revati natives is one way in many cases and they may not expect much or anything in return.

Goddess Saraswati is assigned as another ruling deity of Anuradha. Hence Anuradha associates with all types of learning through goddess Saraswati. Accordingly, Anuradha natives may be skilled in many types of arts like music and singing.

Vedic astrology assigns Saturn as the ruling planet of Anuradha. The influence of Saturn blesses Anuradha with characteristics like practicality, analytical ability, perseverance and discipline. Due to these characteristics, Anuradha natives generally have sensible and no-nonsense approach towards life. Anuradha natives are generally very good at separating the right path from the wrong one.

This characteristic of Anuradha is in contrast to the characteristic of Vishakha, which may often choose the wrong path over the right one. It means natives under strong influence of Anuradha may pay more attention to how a goal should be reached, than reaching the goal itself. For this reason, Anuradha native generally don't deviate from their standard moral behaviors. Hence it may be difficult to lure them to engage in immoral deeds, by showing them various types of rewards.

All quarters of Anuradha fall in Scorpio which is ruled by Mars. Influence of Scorpio and Mars on Anuradha blesses it with abundant energy to pursue and achieve its goals. Influence of Scorpio also adds elements of mystery and the occult to Anuradha, since Scorpio is considered as a sign of mysteries and the occult in Vedic astrology.

Due to the combined effect of these influences on Anuradha, natives under its strong influence are generally very good at making friends and they are capable of achieving success in various fields of their lives by virtue of group work. Anuradha natives may be very good learners. Hence they may learn many different topics and subjects easily, compared to many other nakshatra type natives. When it comes to learn new languages, natives under strong influence of Anuradha may outperform most other nakshatra type natives. Anuradha natives may easily be considered among the quickest learners, in studies as well as in other fields.

Anuradha natives may be especially good in subjects like mathematics and science; and they may be quick at making calculations. Accordingly, many of them may succeed in professional fields where quick calculations are required. Hence natives under strong influence of Anuradha may achieve success as astrologers, mathematicians, scientists, astronomers, researchers, analysts and many other similar types of professionals.

Anuradha natives may be good in the field of communications. They may have natural ability to make friends easily and relate easily to people who belong to different age groups, races or cultures. Anuradha is a promoter of universal brotherhood. Accordingly, Anuradha natives are likely to be connected to people from various religions, countries and beliefs.

Due to influence of Mars and Scorpio on Anuradha, Anuradha natives may be well capable of challenging the outdated traditions of society. Anuradha natives may be capable of setting new traditions and trends for other people to follow. Influences of Saturn and Mitra on Anuradha may bless the natives under its strong impact with the ability to connect to people on mass levels and influence them with their logical reasoning.

Influence of Mars on Anuradha provides sufficient energy to these natives to bring about required changes. Mars is known as a planet of energy and rebellion. Accordingly, natives under strong influence of Anuradha may start revolutions and they may root out old and outdated traditions or systems through such revolutions. It may be easy for Anuradha natives to gain support of people due to influence of Mitra on Anuradha. Hence Anuradha natives may prove good leaders who may start revolutions and see them through.

Drawing a comparison, Ashwini natives are also rebels and they also love to rebel against irrelevant traditions or laws. However, there is significant difference between Ashwini natives and Anuradha natives when it comes to the intention involved, methods used and results achieved, through such rebellions. Ashwini is independent, impulsive, impatient and it believes more in working alone than in groups.

Hence Ashwini natives are more likely to rebel for their own freedom or rights, instead of fighting for the rights of the others, unless this tendency is corrected by other planets in a horoscope. For example, if Ashwini natives are given exemption from obeying a rule, law or tradition, they may not rebel. It should be noted that Ashwini is individualist and not selfish. Ashwini natives are generally not mature enough to understand the needs of society as whole and they are busy handling their own issues.

Ashwini is like a teenager who wants to resolve his problems at the earliest, with little interest in what is happening in the world around him. This teenager is not selfish in doing so; he is simply not grown enough. Hence he wishes to do all that is needed for him to grow up or be happy. In addition to that, Ashwini natives are generally impulsive and impatient.

Therefore, they may rebel, more due to heat of the moments and they may not do so after carefully considering all aspects related to such rebellions or revolutions. Since they may be impatient, Ashwini natives may quit participating in rebellions or revolutions during their courses, and they may move to some other missions, their impulses may ask them to engage in.

It means Ashwini natives may not rebel for society, they may not work well in groups, they may not make elaborate plans before engaging in such acts and they may leave such missions incomplete. All these characteristics make Ashwini natives unfit for leading revolutions or rebellions, though they may be good at participating in them for tasks which require short durations of time.

Looking at natives under strong influence of Anuradha, they are likely to be mature, society oriented, disciplined and dedicated. It means Anuradha natives may start revolutions when they are needed for the benefits of larger groups of people. They may duly plan all aspects of such revolutions and they may work with large groups of people, very likely in leading positions. Due to influences of Mars and Saturn; Anuradha natives may have sufficient energy, patience and dedication to take such missions to the end and win. Hence Anuradha natives are different in the way they rebel, compared to Ashwini natives.

Anuradha natives are also seen to have good interest in fields like astrology, numerology and other paranormal or occult phenomena. Anuradha natives may be keen on learning new things and exploring new worlds. As a result, many of these natives may travel to foreign countries many times in their lives and some of them may settle permanently in foreign countries. Anuradha natives may be blessed with the ability to adjust themselves to completely new surroundings or countries in very short periods of time. Due to this characteristic, they may easily establish themselves in foreign lands and foreign cultures.

Though Anuradha exhibits a number of characteristics, different natives may embrace different characteristics, depending on placements of various planets in this nakshatra; as well as on their overall horoscopes. Among navagraha; Sun, Jupiter, Mars, Saturn and Ketu perform well in Anuradha. Mercury and Venus may perform well in Anuradha when supported by overall horoscopes. Rahu may perform above average in Anuradha under specific conditions, despite the fact that it is debilitated in Scorpio. This is because Rahu is very comfortable in Anuradha. Moon may not perform well in Anuradha since it is debilitated in Scorpio.

Placement of malefic planets in Anuradha in a horoscope may weaken or corrupt the characteristics of this nakshatra, causing various types of problems for the native, depending on his overall horoscope. For example, if a malefic combination of Mars and Rahu forms Angarak Yoga in the first house of a horoscope in Scorpio in Anuradha; and the rest of the horoscope is negative in a specific way; the native may become a terrorist.

Angarak Yoga may corrupt characteristics of Anuradha and the native may engage in acts of rebellion or revolutions, which may not be in tune with universal wellbeing. It means such native may use violence for selfish motives, though he may convince himself that such motives are noble. Since Anuradha is a group oriented nakshatra, such native may work with a terrorist organization, rather than working alone.

One of the biggest differences between a genuine Anuradha type revolutionary and an Anuradha type terrorist is the fact that the former may almost never kill an innocent person, in order to win his wars. On the other hand, Anuradha type terrorist may not hesitate in killing dozens or hundreds of innocent people for his mission, and he may justify such acts of violence as necessary or noble.

A revolutionary is the one who has issues with some specific people or with a system; and he may use violence if needed, against such people or system only. A terrorist is the one who may use violence against anyone to prove his point, even if such people have nothing to do with his problems. When you kill innocent or impartial people, you go against the principal of universal wellbeing. You see, the same characteristic of fighting for justice, exhibited by Anuradha may be entirely misinterpreted and misused, when malefic planets are placed in it.

Let's look at performances of various planets in various navamshas of Anuradha. Starting with Leo navamsha; Mars, Jupiter and Ketu may perform well or very well here, since all of them are strong in Scorpio as well as Leo. Sun may perform above average or well in this navamsha; since it has good strength in Scorpio and it is strong in Leo. Within the sign of Scorpio; Sun may be the strongest in this navamsha.

Mercury and Venus may perform above average in this navamsha, since both of them have fair strength in Leo as well as Scorpio and they are comfortable in Anuradha. Saturn may perform on average here; since it is comfortable in Anuradha but it is not strong in Scorpio and it is weak in Leo.

Moon may perform below average or poorly here; since it is not strong in Leo and debilitated in Scorpio; but it is comfortable in Anuradha. Rahu may perform below average here; since it is debilitated in Scorpio and weak in Leo, but it has great comfort in Anuradha. Among navagraha; Mars and Ketu may be the strongest in this navamsha whereas Moon may be the weakest.

Looking at Virgo navamsha; Mars may perform well or very well here whereas Ketu may perform well but not very well here; since it is debilitated in Virgo. Sun may perform on average here whereas Jupiter may perform above average in this navamsha. Jupiter is stronger than Sun in Scorpio and it is more comfortable than Sun in Anuradha.

Mercury may perform above average here; since it is exalted in Virgo. Saturn may perform well here; since it is strong in Virgo and it is comfortable in Anuradha. Venus may perform on average here; since it has decent strength in Scorpio and it is comfortable in Anuradha, but it is debilitated in Virgo.

Rahu may perform above average in this navamsha, despite being debilitated in Scorpio. Rahu is very comfortable in Anuradha and it is exalted in Virgo. Such placement of Rahu may produce scientists, mathematicians and other likewise professionals. Moon may perform below average or poorly in this navamsha; since it is not strong in Virgo and debilitated in Scorpio. Among navagraha; Mars may be the strongest in this navamsha whereas Moon may be the weakest.

Moving on to Libra navamsha; Mars may perform very well here whereas Jupiter may perform above average or well in this navamsha. Jupiter is very comfortable in Anuradha, it is strong in Scorpio and it has decent strength in Libra. Sun may perform below average in this navamsha. It has good strength in Scorpio but it is not much comfortable in Anuradha and it is debilitated in Libra.

Venus may perform above average or well in this navamsha whereas Saturn may perform well here. Both these planets are comfortable in Anuradha; they have decent strength in Scorpio and they are strong in Libra. Ketu may perform well but not very well in this navamsha; since it is exalted in Scorpio but it is not strong in Libra and it is not much comfortable in Anuradha. Mercury may perform above average here.

Rahu may perform on average or above average in this navamsha; since it is very comfortable in Anuradha and it is strong in Libra; but it is debilitated in Scorpio. Moon may perform below average or poorly in this navamsha; since it is debilitated in Scorpio and it is has decent strength in Libra. Among navagraha; Mars may be the strongest in this navamsha whereas Moon may be the weakest.

Considering Scorpio navamsha; Mars may perform very well here whereas Ketu and Jupiter may perform well or very well here; depending on the overall horoscope. Jupiter is strong in Scorpio though not as strong as Mars and Ketu; and it is very comfortable in Anuradha. Ketu is exalted in Scorpio but not much comfortable in Anuradha. Sun may perform above average in this navamsha since it has good strength in Scorpio but it is not much comfortable in Anuradha.

Mercury may perform on average here whereas Venus and Saturn may perform above average in this navamsha. Mercury may not be as comfortable in Anuradha as Venus and Saturn; though it is comfortable in this nakshatra.

Rahu may perform below average or poorly but not very poorly in this navamsha. Though Rahu is debilitated in its sign of placement as well as in navamsha; it is one of the most comfortable planets in Anuradha. Among navagraha; Rahu and Jupiter may be the most comfortable in Anuradha whereas Mars may be somewhat less comfortable than them in this nakshatra, though it may still be very comfortable. Hence Rahu may not perform very poorly in any navamsha of Anuradha; including this navamsha. Therefore, it may be very weak here but it may still not perform very poorly here.

Moon may perform poorly or very poorly in this navamsha. Moon is debilitated in Scorpio and it is not as comfortable in Anuradha as Rahu. Among navagraha; Mars may be the strongest in this navamsha whereas Moon may be the weakest. Among all 108 navamshas of 27 nakshatras; Moon may be the weakest in this navamsha.

It should be noted that performance of a planet in a nakshatra is different from its comfort in that nakshatra. Performance of a planet in a nakshatra includes the sign/ signs in which such nakshatra is placed and it also includes the navamsha within such nakshatra; where such planet may be placed. On the other hand, comfort of a planet in a nakshatra doesn't include any of these factors, and it is an equation, directly between the planet and nakshatra.

Anuradha is a patient, wise, sharing, friendly, learning, adventurous, kind, generous and social nakshatra which cares about universal wellbeing and which likes to bring about reforms. Looking at comfort of various planets in this nakshatra; Rahu is the best among navagraha; when it comes to learn new languages, visit to foreign places, make new friends and engage in adventures. Hence it has great comfort in Anuradha.

Jupiter also likes learning as well as sharing; and it is very much interested in universal wellbeing. Hence it too has great comfort in Anuradha. Mars may have somewhat less comfort here since it is not patient and wise; though it may be comfortable with most other characteristics of Anuradha. Venus may also be very comfortable in Anuradha since it is a social planet which loves to share.

Saturn is wise and patient; and it strongly believes in harmony. Hence it too may be comfortable in this nakshatra. Since Saturn is not about adventures and learning new things; it may not be as comfortable as Rahu, Jupiter and Mars. Mercury may have problems when it comes to share and it may be impatient at times. However, it may be comfortable with a number of other characteristics of Anuradha. Hence it may be comfortable but not very comfortable in this nakshatra.

Moon may be in alignment with many characteristics of Anuradha but it may not be much comfortable with reforms which may include violence; and some other characteristics. Hence it may be comfortable but not very comfortable in Anuradha.

Sun is all about individualism whereas sharing and being social are prominent characteristics of Anuradha. Hence Sun may not be much comfortable in this nakshatra though it may not have much discomfort also; since it relates to some other characteristics of this nakshatra; like being adventurous and bringing about reforms.

Ketu is happy alone, it may not be interested in learning new things and it may not care much about reforms also. However, it is not strongly opposed to learning and reforms. It may simply not be interested. Hence Ketu may not have much comfort in Anuradha though it may not have much discomfort also.

Looking at professions, natives under strong influence of Anuradha may achieve success as counselors, therapists, psychologists, scientists, researchers, explorers, analysts, environmentalists, astrologers, numerologists, mathematicians, doctors, healers, psychics, tantrics, spiritual gurus, translators, mediators, teachers, preachers, coaches, negotiators, politicians, diplomats, defense professionals and other government officers; singers, musicians, painters, writers, dancers, actors, sportsmen, photographers, professionals dealing in defense related industries, education field, music industry, media industry, social media networks, airline industry, tour and travel industry, shipping industry, hotel industry; and many other types of professionals, depending on their overall horoscopes.

Let's look at some other facts associated with this nakshatra. Anuradha is considered as a passive and tender nakshatra. It is considered as a male nakshatra. Vedic astrology assigns Shudra Varna and fire element to Anuradha. The Gana assigned to Anuradha is Deva and the Guna assigned to it is Tamasic. It is a level nakshatra and its Yoni or animal symbol is Deer.

Jyeshtha

Jyeshtha is 18th among 27 nakshatras. All four quarters of Jyeshtha fall in Scorpio. It marks the completion of the second set of nine nakshatras from Magha to Jyeshtha.

The literal meaning of the word Jyeshtha is 'elder' and Vedic astrology associates the meanings like elder, mature and senior with Jyeshtha. It is believed that natives under strong influence of Jyeshtha may mature early in their lives, both in physical as well as in mental sense. It means Jyeshtha natives may have better senses of social norms compared to many other nakshatra type natives. Hence they may easily understand what drives families, societies, cities and/or states, depending on their ages and circumstances.

Vedic astrology takes the main symbol of Jyeshtha as a Round Talisman which is worn by people for protection from evil forces. Round talismans were also worn by people in authority, in old civilizations. Hence Jyeshtha exhibits characteristics like protection and authority as indicated by its symbol. A talisman is also worn by people who deal in occult or paranormal practices. Hence Jyeshtha also connects to the realms of paranormal and occult through this symbol.

A symbol of Umbrella is also assigned to Jyeshtha. This symbol also associates characteristics like protection and authority with Jyeshtha. An umbrella is used by people to protect themselves from rain or sun. History tells that a kind of big umbrella called Chhatra was used frequently by Kings to convey the idea of protection as well as authority. It means Jyeshtha has lot to do with characteristics like protection, maturity and authority of one type or another.

Vedic astrology assigns Indra, the king of gods as the ruling deity of Jyeshtha. Hence many characteristics of Indra are relayed through Jyeshtha. Indra is portrayed as a cunning, selfish, tricky and proud character in many stories of Vedic mythology. He is also known to misuse his power and authority to achieve his goals. Hence Indra comes across as a character having more negative shades in his personality than the positive ones.

However, Indra also has many good characteristics like protecting his subjects, taking care of them, maintaining law and order; and other characteristics. Many of these characteristics of Indra are exhibited through Jyeshtha. Indra is also the ruling deity of Vishakha and many of his characteristics are relayed through Vishakha. Same is the case with Jyeshtha which also exhibits many characteristics of Indra. Hence Jyeshtha may seem to work like Vishakha in many ways.

However, Jyeshtha is ruled by Mercury, it is influenced by Mars through Scorpio and it is placed in Scorpio which is more interested in understanding things on deeper levels; than in pleasures of various types. It means Jyeshtha wants to go deeper than pleasures of flesh or senses and it wants to understand how the bigger systems work. Jyeshtha wants to understand such systems, in order to be a prominent part of them and in order to gain authority as well as control.

When it comes to Vishakha, natives under its strong influence may be primarily looking for pleasures of senses and all else they may be doing, may be primarily to achieve and sustain such pleasures. On the other hand, natives under strong influence of Jyeshtha may primarily look to establish themselves and have control over a group of people. Depending on the horoscope of one such native, such group may be a family, a community, a city, a state or an entire country.

It has been discussed in Poorvaphalguni that a king has two opposite looking sides. One side is there to rule, expand and protect; whereas the other side is there to enjoy, relax and rejuvenate. Vishakha relays the enjoyment side of Indra whereas Jyeshtha exhibits the ruler side of Indra. Since it is an essential job of the ruler to protect his subjects, Jyeshtha features protection as its prominent characteristic. It should be noted that protection indicated by Jyeshtha has two aspects.

Looking at the first aspect; natives under strong influence of Jyeshtha may be protected by virtue of their characteristics, they may be protected by someone in authority or they may receive such protection through faiths like astrology.

This aspect of protection is indicated by the symbols of Jyeshtha which are a round talisman and an umbrella. Both these symbols show that the native is protected, though in different ways. An umbrella shows protection through skills or authority, since kings used such umbrellas. A talisman indicates protection through some type of paranormal or occult faith, like astrology or tantra. Hence natives under strong influence of Jyeshtha may have interest in faiths like astrology and they may follow these faiths, in order to stay protected.

Looking at the second aspect of protection associated with Jyeshtha, it is the protection offered by Jyeshtha natives to a group of people. It is the job of a ruler to protect and provide. The name Jyeshtha translates into elder and the elders are supposed to protect the younger. Indra as a ruler fought a number of wars with demons, in order to maintain balance. He is also considered as the ruler of rain, and rain means provisions and prosperity.

Hence natives under strong influence of Jyeshtha may protect people dependent on them and they may also provide for them. It means if a family has five members, the one under strong influence of Jyeshtha is likely to assume the lead role in such family with time; even if he is the youngest member. On bigger levels, Jyeshtha natives may protect and provide for societies, cities, states and countries; operating from posts of authority. Therefore, Jyeshtha is quite different from Vishakha, though both of them are ruled by Indra.

Vedic astrology assigns Mercury as the ruling planet of Jyeshtha. Mercury is known for characteristics like intellect, logic, mathematical skills and analytical abilities. Influence of Mercury on Jyeshtha adds these characteristics to Jyeshtha. These characteristics make Jyeshtha a much more stable and balanced nakshatra, compared to Vishakha. All quarters of Jyeshtha fall in Scorpio ruled by Mars. Mars exhibits characteristics like energy, initiative and courage. Scorpio displays characteristics like intensity, insight and high sense of perception. All these characteristic are also added to Jyeshtha.

As a result, Jyeshtha becomes a very capable, gifted, courageous and special type of nakshatra, especially when it comes to supervise and manage materialistic affairs which demand administrative skills and authority. Hence Jyeshtha natives may be gifted with characteristics like administrative skills, management skills and diplomatic skills. They may achieve authority through these characteristics as well as through other characteristics of Jyeshtha and they may use all these characteristics to protect and provide for groups of people; they are supposed to care for.

Therefore, Jyeshtha is a favourite one when it comes to achieve authority and command people, especially through politics. Strong influence of Jyeshtha may bless the natives with very good understanding of individual as well as mass psychology. This characteristic may help them gain authority through politics and it may help them serve better, if such natives get such authority as government officers.

An administrative officer under strong influence of Jyeshtha may be very good at maintaining law and order in the area under his jurisdiction. Such officer may be well aware of most elements which create disturbances and he may also know how to manage such elements. It should be noted that these benefic effects may be witnessed by a native, only when Jyeshtha is occupied by benefic planets in his horoscope or it is rising in the ascendant without any planet in such ascendant.

Placements of malefic planets in Jyeshtha may weaken or corrupt its characteristics. As a result, the native may use these characteristics for selfish motives, instead of using them for higher causes. A corrupt minister, chief minister, prime minister or president under strong negative influence of Jyeshtha may go to any lengths to maintain his position of authority.

These may be some of the most difficult people to deal with as well as to get rid of. Such politicians may understand the psychology of masses very well and they may also be skilled at the art of projecting themselves as genuine leaders. Hence they may keep engaging in various types of corrupt and immoral deeds but the public may not be able to see their real faces. A head of state who gets a high authority politician assassinated and then announces national holiday in his honor, is very like to be a Jyeshtha type head of state.

Jyeshtha natives generally mature earlier than many other nakshatra types. In many cases, this maturity is more of mental and psychic type, than physical type. Jyeshtha natives may be clever and they may be capable of making decisions based on facts and logics. Jyeshtha natives are generally very concerned about how they are perceived by other people. To maintain status and image in society may be important for them. Jyeshtha natives may try their best to ensure that their public images remain good, even if they are engaging in wrong deeds, due to overall negative horoscopes.

These natives may be good at hiding their inner feelings and intentions. They may also be good at acting or projecting themselves to be the ones they may not be. A number of politicians in present times may be under strong influence of Jyeshtha. Such politicians may be very well capable of keeping their public images clean. Such politicians may be perceived to have good characters, which they may or may not have. Even if such Jyeshtha type politicians actually have good characters, they may put a lot of effort to project and maintain good pubic images.

It should be noted that having good character is one thing and desiring to be perceived good by others is another. Looking at a contrast, natives under strong influence of Uttarabhadrapada or Revati may have very good and noble characters, when supported by overall horoscopes. However, these natives may not bother about being perceived good and they may be content, simply in being good. Hence they may keep doing their respective jobs and they may not engage in any efforts to highlight their good deeds. On the other hand, even some of the best Jyeshtha natives may have strong tendency to get their good deeds noticed.

For instance, a native under strong influence of Uttarabhadrapada may make an anonymous donation worth in millions or more. For this native, the act of donation matters and nothing else may. On the other hand, a native under strong influence of Jyeshtha may almost always make such donation through a highly official platform. It means he may ensure that he is covered by news and he is given due credit and respect for being a generous donor.

It should be noted that such Jyeshtha native may also be a very good person, as it takes goodness to engage in such acts of generosity. However, he may be less evolved compared to Uttarabhadrapada native who may be a believer of engaging in good karmas without any desires for fruits of any type. For natives under strong benefic influence of Jyeshtha, the desire for fruits may almost always be there.

Jyeshtha natives are generally good at performing their duties. They believe in doing their duties in disciplined and timely manners. Jyeshtha natives may be good at helping other people and they may sometimes go out of way in order to help the needy. At times, natives under strong benefic influence of Jyeshtha may pick up fights with people or organizations much bigger than them, in order to protect people who are weak and who cannot protect themselves. Jyeshtha natives are generally justice loving people and they try to balance things in just ways. However, they may bend some rules when they have themselves committed injustice or their dear ones have.

Jyeshtha natives may have significant amount of faith in astrology and other paranormal phenomena. Many Jyeshtha natives may resort to such faiths, in order to grow more and stay protected. These natives also have tendency to choose some occult science as their field of profession. Hence some natives under strong influence of Jyeshtha may practice as astrologers, psychics, tantrics, healers and spiritual gurus. Jyeshtha has a significant tendency to be associated with some element of mystery and occult. This is because all quarters of Jyeshtha fall in Scorpio which is considered as the sign associated with mysteries and the occult.

Since they may have good or very good understanding of human psychology, they may also succeed as various types of consultants who may help people or groups of people resolve their issues. Psychiatrists under strong influence of Jyeshtha may be very good at understanding the root causes of the problems of their patients. Hence their success rates may be higher in comparison to many other nakshatra type psychiatrists.

Drawing a comparison, a native under strong influence of Ashlesha may become a psychiatrist but a psychiatrist under strong influence of Jyeshtha may go deeper than him, in most cases. Compared to them, a Shatabhisha type psychiatrist may go even deeper. An Uttarabhadrapada type psychiatrist may be better than all of them; since he may go even deeper than the Shatabhisha type psychiatrist.

The Uttarabhadrapada type psychiatrist may not only be very good at going very deep; he may be blessed with the best healing abilities among all four types of natives. It means that his aura may have much more positive impact on his patients. Hence they may be much more convinced by him and they may be motivated to act upon whatever he says. Such invisible healing tendency may be the highest in Uttarabhadrapada natives; followed by Jyeshtha, Shatabhisha and Ashlesha respectively.

It means that though Shatbhisha native may have deeper understanding of core issues of his patients than Jyeshtha native; the latter may have better healing abilities. Shatabhisha native may have to do much convincing in order to make his patients follow him whereas Jyeshtha native may have to work less hard in doing so; as some invisible force may encourage his patients to believe in him and follow him.

This force may be the strongest in case of Uttarabhadrapada native who may heal many patients; merely with his words and presence. Ashlesha native may have to put maximum amount of work in order to get results and he may not receive much invisible help. It should be noted that though an Ashlesha native may not perform as well as Jyeshtha, Shatabhisha and Uttarabhadrapada native as a psychiatrist; he may perform better than many other nakshatra type natives; who may practice as psychiatrists.

Though Jyeshtha exhibits a number of characteristics, different natives may embrace different characteristics, depending on placements of various planets in this nakshatra, as well as on their overall horoscopes. Looking at planets; Sun, Jupiter, Mars, Venus, Mercury, Saturn, Rahu and Ketu are comfortable in Jyeshtha, though they have different levels of comfort. Moon feels uncomfortable in Jyeshtha.

Placements of malefic planets in Jyeshtha may weaken or corrupt its characteristics. As a result, the native may suffer from a wide variety of problems, depending on his overall horoscope. Taking an example, if a malefic combination of debilitated Moon, Rahu and Saturn is placed in the fourth house of a horoscope in Scorpio in Jyeshtha, the native may suffer from significant psychological problems.

At the same time, if a malefic combination of Sun and retrograde exalted Jupiter is placed in the twelfth house of this horoscope in Cancer in Ashlesha, the problem may worsen. Such native may suffer from serious psychological problems and he may spend many years of his life in a mental asylum. If there are no grace saving planets in his horoscope, the native may die in a mental asylum.

Let's look at performances of various planets in various navamshas of Jyeshtha. Starting with Sagittarius navamsha; Mars, Jupiter and Ketu may do well or very well here since they are all strong in Scorpio as well as Sagittarius. Among these three; Jupiter may deliver best results in this navamsha; provided it is benefic in the horoscope under consideration.

Sun may perform well in this navamsha whereas Saturn may perform on average or above average here. Sun has good strength in Scorpio, it is strong in Sagittarius and it is very comfortable in Jyeshtha. Saturn is not strong in Scorpio, it is not strong in Sagittarius and it is very comfortable in Jyeshtha.

Venus may perform on average or below average here whereas Mercury may perform on average or above average in this navamsha. Mercury is very comfortable in Jyeshtha but it is not strong in Sagittarius as well as Scorpio.

Rahu and Moon may perform poorly in this navamsha. Rahu is very comfortable in Jyeshtha but it is debilitated in Scorpio and weak in Sagittarius. Moon is debilitated in Scorpio, it has decent strength in Sagittarius and it is not comfortable in Jyeshtha. Among navagraha; Mars may be the strongest here whereas Moon and Rahu may be the weakest.

Looking at Capricorn navamsha; Mars may perform very well here whereas Ketu may perform well or very well in this navamsha. Mars is strong in Scorpio and exalted in Capricorn whereas Ketu is exalted in Scorpio and it has decent strength in Capricorn. Sun may perform above average here whereas Jupiter may perform on average or above average here; since it is debilitated in Capricorn.

Saturn and Mercury may perform above average or well here whereas Venus may perform above average in this navamsha. All these planets are not strong in Scorpio and they are strong in Capricorn. However, Venus is less comfortable in Jyeshtha; compared to Saturn and Mercury.

Rahu may perform on average or below average here whereas Moon may perform below average or poorly in this navamsha. Rahu is strong in Capricorn and it is very comfortable in Jyeshtha whereas Moon has decent strength in Capricorn and it is not comfortable in Jyeshtha. Among navagraha; Mars may be the strongest in this navamsha whereas Moon may be the weakest.

Moving on to Aquarius navamsha; Mars and Ketu may do well or very well here whereas Jupiter may do well but not very well in this navamsha. Jupiter is not as strong in Scorpio as Mars and Ketu; and all these planets are not strong in Aquarius.

Saturn and Mercury may perform above average or well here whereas Venus may perform above average in this navamsha. All these planets are not strong in Scorpio and they are strong in Aquarius. However, Venus is less comfortable in Jyeshtha; compared to Saturn and Mercury.

Rahu may perform on average here whereas Moon may perform poorly or very poorly in this navamsha. Rahu is strong in Aquarius and it is very comfortable in Jyeshtha whereas Moon is weak in Aquarius and it is not comfortable in Jyeshtha. Among navagraha; Mars may be the strongest in this navamsha whereas Moon may be the weakest.

Considering Pisces navamsha; Mars, Jupiter and Ketu may do well or very well here. Mars is not as strong as Jupiter in Pisces but it is stronger than Jupiter in Scorpio. Among these three; Ketu may be the strongest in this navamsha since it is exalted in Scorpio as well as Pisces. Sun may perform above average in this navamsha since it is not strong in Pisces.

Venus may perform above average but not well here. Though it is exalted in Pisces; it is not strong in Scorpio and it is not very comfortable in Jyeshtha. Saturn may perform on average here whereas Mercury may perform below average in this navamsha. Saturn is not strong in Pisces whereas Mercury is debilitated in this sign.

Moon may perform poorly in this navamsha though it is strong in Pisces. This is because Moon forms Gandmool Dosh in this navamsha of Jyeshtha. Rahu may perform poorly or very poorly in this navamsha. Rahu is very comfortable in Jyeshtha but it is debilitated in Scorpio as well as Pisces. Within the sign of Scorpio; Rahu may be the weakest in this navamsha. Among navagraha; Ketu may be the strongest here whereas Rahu may be the weakest.

Looking at professions, natives under strong influence of Jyeshtha may achieve success as politicians, diplomats, manipulators, power brokers and other such professionals practicing in similar fields; administrators, government officers, police offices, army officers, naval officers, astrologers, numerologists, psychics, palmists, black magicians, tantrics, healers, doctors, engineers, lawyers, judges, bankers, researchers, explorers, consultants, psychiatrists, managers, mediators, writers, singers, professionals dealing in event management industry, private security, media industry, ecommerce, weapon making industry, industries dealing in all types of security equipment, financial sector, real estate sector and many other types of professionals, depending on their overall horoscopes.

Let's look at some other facts associated with this nakshatra. Jyeshtha is considered as an active and harsh nakshatra. It is considered as a female nakshatra. Vedic astrology assigns Servant Varna and air element to Jyeshtha. The Gana assigned to Jyeshtha is Rakshasa and the Guna assigned to it is Sattwic. It is a level nakshatra and its Yoni or animal symbol is male Deer.

Moola

Moola is 19th among 27 nakshatras. All four quarters of Moola fall in Sagittarius. It marks the beginning of the third set of nakshatras ranging from Moola to Revati.

The literal translation for the word Moola is 'root'. Root is the most important and the innermost part of a plant or tree. A root also conveys the sense of being grounded and holding. The ability to look at the root of a matter means recognizing the most important aspect of an issue. Significant amount of curiosity, intelligence and energy is required to reach to the root of a matter.

Root of anything is as deep as it gets. Hence such root indicates the approach to look at things as they are in their purest forms. Combining all these attributes, Moola exhibits characteristics like being rooted, curiosity, intelligence, energy and direct or straight forward approach in dealing with issues.

Vedic astrology assigns a tied bunch of roots as the main symbol of Moola. This tied bunch of roots again conveys various meanings. A tied bunch of roots indicates variety, versatility and strength through unity. Hence Moola exhibits characteristics like versatility and strength through union. It means natives under strong influence of Moola may be good at connecting with their roots and they may gain strength through such connections.

Hence Moola natives may have closely formed bonds with their parents, siblings, relatives and childhood friends; and these relationships may be at the root of their strength. A connection with roots also suggests affinity with family line. Accordingly, natives under strong influence of Moola may feel deeply connected to their ancestral lineage and family traditions. Moola natives may be straight forward in their approach and they may not care for social norms. It means a Moola native may say things as he sees them and he may not care about the kind of reactions his words may bring back.

Since Moola natives may be gifted with the ability to reach to the root of matters; their speech patterns may often offend other people. This is because they may not only speak out loud when they find something is bad, they may also tell why it is bad. For many people, adding the root cause may only mean adding insult to injury. For example, a Moola native may say something like, 'this dark yellow doesn't suit you because of your dark complexion'.

Though this Moola native may be telling the truth according to his understanding; he may be hitting the affected person with double strength. The first blow is that dark yellow doesn't suit him and the second blow is that his complexion is dark. Though it is an honest comment according to such Moola native, the other person may get offended.

Taking a look at another example, a native under strong influence of Moola may say, 'the food is too salty today and it is overcooked'. Once again, it is an honest comment according to such Moola native but it may seriously offend the other person. Due to such straight forward approach, Moola natives may often be called outspoken or even offensive.

It should be noted that Moola natives may also be good at giving complements and that too with details. For example, a Moola native may say, 'you look beautiful today and this new hair style enhances your beauty'. Hence Moola natives may be straight forward with their approach though such attitude may often cause problems for them, unless there are corrective planets in their horoscopes.

Such direct approach may not be limited to their speech or opinions and it may also reflect through their actions. For example, a Moola native may reject a girl on her face on the first date, if he finds she is not a good match for her. A Rohini native or a Poorvaphalguni native in this situation may simply make an excuse and leave the venue; without saying anything to the girl; and he may never date the girl again. However, a Moola native in the same situation may tell her that she is not fit for him and hence they should not date again. Though such Moola native may be speaking the truth in this case also, to the best of his knowledge; he may be perceived as offensive.

Due to such straight forward approach, Moola natives may not believe in formalities and they may directly deal with the issues at hand. For example, a Moola native may go to his neighbor and directly ask for his car in case of need, without exchanging any courtesies. Such Moola native may say, 'my car is broken, can I borrow your car for today'. If the neighbor gives him the key, such native may say a simple thanks and leave. He may not bother about exchanging any courtesies before asking for car and after getting such car.

Looking at this equation from the opposite angle, if the neighbor comes and asks for his car, the reaction may again be straight forward. Such Moola native may bring the key and give it to the neighbor, without even asking him to come in or offering him a drink. Hence Moola natives may lack diplomatic skills and they may often face problems due to their direct to the point approach. For this reason, Moola natives may be perceived as outspoken, harsh and rude; though they may simply not care.

Roots are directly related to strength of trees or plants they represent. It means various plants having roots receive strength and growth through roots. Hence stronger are the roots, stronger is the tree or plant. Accordingly, natives under strong influence of Moola may try to achieve power and authority in their lives and they may take help from their roots in order to do so.

For example, a native under strong influence of Moola may ask his father for business investment, so that he may achieve more growth in profession. Compared to this, a native under strong influence of Ardra may not do so and even if his father himself offers help, such Ardra native may refuse. This is because Ardra believes more in achieving success through its own efforts.

It should be noted that the root of a plant or tree is always hidden and it is covered in mystery. Hence Moola natives have tendency to connect to the hidden, mysterious and occult side of nature. Therefore many Moola natives may resort to faiths like astrology or tantra, in order to gain success and power.

Some natives under strong and specific influence of Moola may also engage in professions related to such fields. These natives may become astrologers, tantrics, psychics, spiritual gurus and other such professionals; depending on their overall horoscopes. Since roots are always hidden in mystery, this characteristic may also be exhibited by Moola. It means natives under strong influence of Moola may be skilled at hiding their strengths, their sources of power and their intentions.

Vedic astrology assigns Nritti as the ruling deity of Moola. Nritti is considered as the goddess of destruction according to Vedic mythology as the word Nritti literally translates into Calamity or destruction on a large scale. Accordingly, many characteristics of Nritti like the ability to destruct, aggression, anger and violence are relayed through Moola. These characteristics make Moola a difficult to handle nakshatra.

As a result, placements of unsuitable or malefic planets in Moola in a horoscope may cause serious problems for the native as well as for other people. It should be noted that destruction represented by Nritti is on large scale. It means natives under strong influence of Moola are capable of waging wars and other such acts; which may end up causing destruction on large scales.

For this reason, many Vedic astrologers fear Moola and they paint it in very bad colours. However, any type of energy in its purest form is innocent and it doesn't have a wish of its own. It means whether the characteristics of Moola are used in accordance with universal theme or such characteristics are used for selfish motives; depends on the overall horoscope of the native under consideration.

Vedic astrology assigns Ketu as the ruling planet of Moola. Ketu is known as a planet associated with past, mysteries, troubles and destruction. Many such characteristics of Ketu are relayed through Moola and they make it an even more difficult to handle nakshatra. Ketu is known as a fiery planet and it has the characteristic of bringing good or bad results in short periods of time. It means the fire of Ketu may cause destruction in no time.

These characteristics of Ketu are also exhibited through Moola, making it a more fearsome nakshatra. Due to all these characteristics exhibited by Moola, natives under its strong influence may have strong urge to destroy. Whether such urge is converted into positive destruction or negative destruction depends on placements of benefic or malefic planets in Moola as well as on the overall horoscope of the native under consideration.

All four quarters of Moola fall in Sagittarius which is a fiery sign ruled by Jupiter. Sagittarius is considered as a lucky, optimistic and prosperous sign. Jupiter is known as the greatest of all natural benefic planets. Therefore, influences of Jupiter and Sagittarius add characteristics like optimism, faith, prosperity, intelligence, creativity and positive outlook to Moola.

These much needed characteristics tend to bring Moola back to balance. This way, Moola becomes a battlefield for conflicting characteristics of different energies. Some of these characteristics look very good whereas some others look horrible. Due to such conflicting characteristics, Moola is one of the most difficult to handle nakshatras, among all 27 nakshatras. Therefore, whether the energy of Moola is used positively or it is used negatively, largely depends on the overall horoscope of a native under its strong influence.

Let's discuss the horoscope of Adolf Hitler, who had strong influence of Moola as well as other malefic energies on him. As a result, he became the root cause of mass destruction, through war as well as through other extreme methods. A malefic combination of Moon in Moola and Jupiter as well as Ketu in Poorvashada is placed in the twelfth house of his horoscope in Sagittarius. Hence Guru Chandal Yoga as well as Grahan Yoga is formed in the twelfth house of his horoscope.

A combination of exalted Sun, Mercury, Mars and retrograde Venus is placed in the fourth house in Aries. Benefic Saturn is placed in the seventh house in Cancer in Ashlesha; and malefic Rahu is placed in the sixth house in

Gemini. Mars is placed in Bharani nakshatra. The first thing to note in this horoscope is that seven out of nine planets are placed in fiery signs, indicating too much fire. Here also, all fiery planets Sun, Mars and Ketu are placed in fiery signs, adding even more fire.

This makes the native significantly impulsive and aggressive. Saturn being the lord of ascendant is placed in the seventh house in Ashlesha which is perfect for rise through politics; as already discussed in chapter named Ashlesha. Mars forms Ruchaka Yoga in the fourth house.

Since the horoscope is strong due to Sun and Mars in Aries and due to Jupiter in Sagittarius; supported by Saturn in Ashlesha; the native rose to power through politics. Mars being the planet of wars is placed in Bharani which is fierce and extreme. Looking into the twelfth house, placement of Moon in Moola is a troublesome placement. Placement of Ketu in the same house aggravates the situation as Ketu is associated with destruction.

Addition of malefic Jupiter to the same house further aggravates the problem. Jupiter deals with religion and races; and Ketu corrupts its significances by afflicting it. Due to this troublesome combination, the native started war with the intention to destroy a race, which he thought was inferior and had no right to live. Hence the native waged war in order to prove superiority of his race over the others, indicating corruption of Jupiter's significances.

Both Ketu and Jupiter are placed in Poorvashada, which stands for being 'invincible'. Hence the native had strong conviction that he is invincible. Poorvashada is also known to be most persistent nakshatra and it may go to the limits of obsession in order to achieve its goals. Accordingly, the native engaged in monumental efforts to achieve his goal. The native had problems with a race and he wanted to root it out, under combined influence of Moola and Guru Chandal Yoga.

Since Moola, Bharani, Mars and Ketu love war and among them; Moola and Ketu have affinity for destruction, the native caused destruction. Moola is known to cause mass destruction and the same happened. The twelfth house deals with prisons and refugee camps among other things. Hence he got a large number of people captured in such camps as prisoners; and he got them killed.

Even when the native started losing, and winning armies marched into the capital, he kept believing that his side was winning. This shows the height of obsession exhibited by Poorvashada. In the end, the native committed suicide as he preferred death over defeat; a typical characteristic of Poorvashada.

Let's now look at an example of the opposite type to understand the working of Moola in an even better way. The name Paramahamsa Yogananda is a highly respected name in spiritual domain. A benefic combination of Sun and Mercury is placed in the fifth house of his horoscope in Sagittarius, forming Budhaditya Yoga. Mercury is placed in Moola and Sun is placed in Poorvashada. Moon is placed in the first house in Leo in Magha, Saturn is placed in the second house in Virgo, Rahu is placed in the ninth house in Aries, Ketu is placed in the third house in Libra, Venus is placed in the fourth house in Scorpio in Jyeshtha; and a combination of Jupiter and Mars is placed in the eighth house in Pisces.

Since Mercury is placed with lord of ascendant, it has significant influence on the native. The fifth house is related to spiritual growth among other things. Moola connects to roots or lineage. Placement of Moon in Magha also indicates authority gained through ancestors, where ancestors in this case are from spiritual lineage, since Moon rules the twelfth house. It means these ancestors are not his physical ancestors and they are his spiritual ancestors. It further means that the native might have been with them during his previous life also.

Hence the native was blessed to be a part of a spiritual lineage filled with highly evolved spiritual souls. Placement of Mars with Jupiter in the eighth house in Pisces indicates spiritual war, the one which is fought within. The eighth house deals with death and this war is fought to achieve victory over death; meaning liberation. Placement of benefic Venus in Jyeshtha indicates authority and dealing with supernatural or the occult.

The combined influence of these energies made this horoscope go in positive direction. Hence the characteristic of destruction exhibited by Moola was used to destroy the demons within, which means the impurities. The native destroyed his impurities with the help of Moola's energy and he reached his original root, the soul. Placement of Rahu in the ninth house in Aries took this native abroad for spiritual teachings. Since the overall horoscope is benefic and strong, the native was able to make best use of energy of Moola.

It means the energy of Moola may be used to destroy millions of innocent people or it may be used to destroy the demons within; depending on the overall horoscope of the native under consideration. Hence Moola may be a difficult to handle energy; but energy in itself is not good or bad; its use is.

Moola natives are generally very focused on their goals. They may keep trying until they have achieved their goals or they have completely exhausted themselves. Moola natives may be neither troubled nor bothered by hindrances on the way and they may keep moving relentlessly to achieve their goals. Moola is an impulsive nakshatra due to strong influences of Ketu and Nritti on it. Hence it may be very quick in taking actions, many times without proper consideration. As a result, Moola natives may have to suffer in the end. However, Moola natives may not learn from their mistakes and they may keep repeating same mistakes.

Moola natives may have good sense of financial management and they may spend their resources wisely. In its extreme form, this tendency may make them spend as little as possible. Hence they may try to save as much money as they can and they may not be willing to spend it; even when it should be. As a result, they may end up creating a number of problems; especially in the sphere of relationships.

When Moola is occupied by malefic planets, these natives may exploit their friends, relatives and allies for selfish motives. Moola natives may also have strong tendency to cut off the ones who they think have become useless for them. Due to this characteristic, Moola natives may often be considered as selfish. Moola natives may be proud and adamant. Such characteristics like being selfish, proud and adamant may bring their downfalls, unless there are corrective planets in their horoscopes.

Moola natives may develop habit of picking fights with others, whenever their egos are hurt. This habit may contribute a lot in bringing their downfalls since they may at times pick fights with people who may cause them serious damage. To summarize, Moola is a difficult to handle nakshatra. Hence natives under strong influence of Moola must have strong supportive horoscopes or else, they may end up using this energy for selfish motives. Such practices may ultimately bring their downfalls and they may have to face serious consequences.

As always, Moola displays a number of characteristics. However, different natives may embrace different characteristics, depending on placements of various planets in this nakshatra as well as on their overall horoscopes. Looking at planets among navagraha; Sun, Mars, Jupiter, Saturn, Rahu and Ketu may handle the energy of Moola with ease. Mercury and Venus may perform well in Moola, under specific conditions.

Moon is not suited for Moola and its placement in this nakshatra may form Gandmool Dosh in horoscope. Gandmool Dosh may prove troublesome for native's own life or for his mother's life; depending on his overall horoscope. Placements of malefic planets in Moola may weaken or corrupt its characteristics. As a result, the native may suffer from a number of problems, depending on his overall horoscope.

Let's look at performances of various planets in various navamshas of Moola. Starting with Aries navamsha; Jupiter, Mars, Sun and Ketu may perform well or very well here; when supported by overall horoscope. All these planets are strong in Sagittarius as well as Aries. Saturn may perform on average or below average in this navamsha; since it is not strong in Sagittarius and it is debilitated in Aries.

Venus may perform on average or above average here whereas Mercury may perform on average in this navamsha. Both Mercury and Venus are not strong in Sagittarius as well as Aries. Rahu may perform on average in this navamsha. Though it is weak in Sagittarius and it is not strong in Aries; it is very comfortable in Moola. Moon forms Gandmool Dosh in this navamsha. Hence it may perform poorly here. Among navagraha; Jupiter may be the strongest in this navamsha whereas Saturn may be the weakest. Moon is not weak in this navamsha but it is troubled.

Looking at Taurus navamsha; Jupiter, Sun and Mars may perform well or very well here whereas Ketu may perform well but not very well in this navamsha. Ketu is strong in Sagittarius and it has great comfort in Moola but it is debilitated in Taurus. Saturn may perform above average in this navamsha since it is strong in Taurus.

Mercury may perform above average here whereas Venus may perform above average or well in this navamsha; since Venus is stronger than Mercury in Taurus. Rahu may perform above average in this navamsha; since it is weak in Sagittarius but it is exalted in Taurus. Moon may perform on average or above average but not well in this navamsha. Though Moon has decent strength in Sagittarius and it is exalted in Taurus; it is not comfortable in Moola. Among navagraha; Jupiter may be the strongest in this navamsha. No planet may be significantly weak in this navamsha.

Moving on to Gemini navamsha; Jupiter, Sun and Mars may do well or very well here whereas Ketu may do well but not very well in this navamsha; since Ketu is weak in Gemini. Saturn may perform on average or above average here; since it is strong in Gemini.

Mercury may perform above average in this navamsha whereas Venus may perform on average or above average here. Venus is stronger than Mercury in Sagittarius whereas Mercury is stronger than Venus in Gemini. Mercury is more comfortable in Moola than Venus. Rahu may perform above average in this navamsha whereas Moon may perform on average or below average here. Among navagraha; Jupiter may be the strongest in this navamsha. No planet may be significantly weak in this navamsha.

Considering Cancer navamsha; Jupiter may perform very well here, Ketu may perform well or very well here;

and Sun as well as Mars may perform well but not very well in this navamsha. Jupiter is exalted in Cancer, Ketu has decent strength in this sign, Sun is weak in Cancer and Mars is debilitated in this sign. Saturn may perform on average in this navamsha; since it is not strong in Sagittarius as well as Cancer.

Venus may perform on average or above average here whereas Mercury may perform on average or below average in this navamsha. Venus has decent strength in Cancer whereas Mercury is weak in this sign. Rahu may perform below average in this navamsha since it is not strong in Sagittarius as well as Cancer. Moon may perform above average here. This may be the easiest to handle navamsha of Moola; due to cooling influence of Cancer. Among navagraha; Jupiter may be the strongest and Rahu may be the weakest in this navamsha.

Looking at professions, natives under strong influence of Moola may be seen practicing as kings, heads of states, dictators, administrators, powerful political leaders, police officers, army officers, air force officers, naval officers, astrologers, psychics, tantrics, exorcists, healers, spiritual gurus, historians, librarians, doctors and especially surgeons, dentists, lawyers, judges, scientists, analysts, IT professionals, sportsmen, gangsters, criminals, arms dealers, murderers, professional killers, serial killers, militants, professionals who sell weapons of mass destruction, drug dealers, pest controllers, professionals dealing in weapon and arms industry, chemical industry, pharmaceutical industry, gardening industry, pest control industry and many other types of professionals, depending on their overall horoscopes.

Let's look at some other facts associated with this nakshatra. Moola is considered as an active and harsh nakshatra. It is considered as neutral in gender. Vedic astrology assigns Butcher Varna and air element to Moola. The Gana assigned to Moola is Rakshasa and the Guna assigned to it is Tamasic. It is a downward nakshatra and its Yoni or animal symbol is Dog.

Poorvashada

Poorvashada is 20th among 27 nakshatras. All four quarters of Poorvashada fall in Sagittarius. The literal translation of the word Poorvashada is 'the former invincible one' or 'the former undefeated one'. Vedic astrology associates Poorvashada with characteristics like being invincible or undefeated.

Poorvashada has its influence on a number of people across the globe and not all of them are invincible. Therefore, the word invincibility is likely to be related to invincibility of mind more than anything else. It means natives under strong influence of Poorvashada may be mentally very strong and they may not accept defeat even under the worst circumstances.

Poorvashada natives may keep trying to achieve their goals, whatever such goals may be. Poorvashada natives may work patiently for very long periods of time to achieve their goals. Poorvashada is capable of fighting for its goals, longer than most other nakshatra types. Even when all else around them has fallen, Poorvashada natives may keep marching forward.

The phrase 'last man standing' applies to Poorvashada in a sense. It means even if a soldier under strong influence of Poorvashada is the last one left and all others have died or run away, he may keep fighting till the end. For this native, war is not over till he wins or dies. In the deepest sense, this is what the word invincibility may be referring to.

A person is not defeated until he accepts defeat. Poorvashada soldier may choose to win or die. Even if he dies, he is not defeated in the deepest sense. Defeat comes from acceptance of the fact that you can't fight any longer or you don't wish to fight any longer due to fear of enemy. Poorvashada natives may keep fighting till they win, they die or there is no war left. Hence they are invincible in this sense.

Some literatures of Vedic astrology assign an alternate name Aparajita for Poorvashada. The literal meaning of the word Aparajita is 'the one who has never been defeated', which means undefeated. Therefore, many Vedic astrologers associate Poorvashada with the characteristic of being undefeated. Hence natives under strong influence of Poorvashada may not accept defeat and they may not give up to failures. Instead, they may keep working hard towards their goals. Many times, Poorvashada natives may be able to achieve their goals, primarily due to this characteristic possessed by them.

Vedic astrology assigns the main symbol of Poorvashada as a hand held fan. Such fan can be used for various purposes and accordingly it represents many characteristics of Poorvashada. A handheld fan is used for cooling and providing relief when it is hot outside. It means Poorvashada has the ability to keep its cools during hot or tough times; by virtue of its patience.

A handheld fan needs constant effort in order to achieve desired result. Hence Poorvashada natives may work constantly, in order to achieve their objectives. A handheld fan can be used to cool other people also. It means Poorvashada natives may be able to cheer up people around them, by virtue of characteristics possessed by them, even when circumstances look bad.

Some centuries ago, a type of handheld fan was used to fan up a fire. Since doing so is an act of aggression, Poorvashada natives may have their due share of aggression. This act also means that Poorvashada has the ability to keep a fire burning by fanning it. This means Poorvashada natives may have the ability to keep the fire inside them alive for long periods of time. They may do so by fanning it with their strong will power and ambitions. These characteristics may help them put up longer and sustained efforts to achieve their goals. Sometimes, a handheld fan is also used to hide face or to conceal identity. Hence it is believed that Poorvashada exhibits the characteristic of hiding things, when it finds necessary.

Vedic astrology assigns Apah, a goddess of water as the ruling deity of Poorvashada. Apah is known as a mysterious and secretive goddess and these characteristics of Apah are relayed through Poorvashada. This makes Poorvashada a secretive, mysterious and hiding type of nakshatra. Apah is also considered as a goddess who is kind at heart but who can be harsh and cruel in her actions when the circumstances demand so.

Therefore, Poorvashada natives can be harsh and cruel when the situation demands them to be so. Whether these characteristics are used positively or negatively; depends on placements of benefic or malefic planets in Poorvashada in a horoscope. When Poorvashada is occupied by malefic planets in a horoscope, the native may use these characteristics for selfish motives.

However when Poorvashada is occupied by suitable benefic planets in a horoscope, the native may use these characteristic for unselfish and bigger purposes. For example, a king or a judge has to be harsh and cruel when he announces death sentence for a murderer. Likewise an army officer or soldier has to be cruel and harsh, when he is killing soldiers of enemy army which has invaded his land. Since both these acts use harshness and cruelty in order to restore balance, these characteristics of Poorvashada are being used positively. Looking at the opposite end of this spectrum, the murderer and the invader may be under strong influence of malefic planets in Poorvashada. This is because both of them are using characteristics like harshness and cruelty for selfish motives.

Vedic astrology assigns Venus as the ruling deity of Poorvashada. Many characteristics of Venus like beauty, glamour, enjoyment, fine taste, creativity and sharing are relayed through Poorvashada. Influence of Venus on Poorvashada adds desire and love for materialistic pursuits to it.

All four quarters of Poorvashada fall in Sagittarius ruled by Jupiter. Characteristics of Jupiter and Sagittarius like hope, optimism, faith, intelligence, creativity, confidence and initiative are expressed through Poorvashada. Jupiter and Venus are two of the most auspicious planets among navagraha and they have their own ways of living and enjoying life to the fullest.

Among 27 nakshatras, only two nakshatras feature combinations of energies of Jupiter and Venus; Vishakha and Poorvashada. These two nakshatras exhibits many characteristics which are similar and some of their characteristics are different.

Comparing these nakshatras, Vishakha is known for fulfilling its desires and living life to the fullest, especially in the sense of physical pleasures. Poorvashada also loves life and it believes in enjoying it to the fullest. However, Poorvashada is not limited to pleasures of physical senses only and it may apply this theory to almost all other spheres of life. Vishakha is a goal oriented nakshatra and nothing or no one may distract it when it sets a target. In order to achieve goals, Vishakha may often end up engaging in immoral or bad deeds.

However, this tendency is more controlled in Poorvashada and it may engage in immoral or bad acts; only when occupied by malefic planets. This is because a number of negative characteristics of Indra are exhibited through Vishakha. Hence Vishakha may not care much for morals, even when it may be occupied by benefic planets in a horoscope. On the other hand, Apah the ruling deity of Poorvashada is not associated with characteristics like selfishness and immorality. On the other hand, she is kind at heart.

The first three quarters of Vishakha fall in Libra which is an air sign and it doesn't help much in making decisions. Due to inability to decide which path is right or wrong, Vishakha may often end up choosing the wrong one. It should be noted that the desire element is very strong in Vishakha which makes it fixate on its goals. The discrimination part is not strong due to influence of Libra. Hence the combination of characteristics like strong desire and lack of discrimination may often lead Vishakha to wrong paths.

On the other hand, Sagittarius is a fiery sign, known for characteristics like initiative, intelligence and discrimination. It means though the desire element may be strong in Poorvashada, it may not often choose wrong paths; since it is capable of separating right from wrong. Therefore, Poorvashada is more balanced in its approach than Vishakha.

A variety of wonderful characteristics are added by Jupiter and Venus to Poorvashada, making it one and only of its kind.

Jupiter and Venus are two of the most resourceful, cheerful, fortunate and life-loving planets among navagraha. All such characteristics of Jupiter and Venus bless Poorvashada with the ability to live life to the fullest. Therefore, Poorvashada may rank at the top when it comes to the art of living life to the fullest. Poorvashada natives may be good at sucking delight from each and every moment of their lives.

Due to combined influence of Jupiter and Venus; Poorvashada natives may prefer to look at what they have, rather than looking at what they don't have. Here also, Vishakha may be capable of enjoying; only what it desires and it may not care much for other things. On the other hand, Poorvashada is capable of enjoying anything and everything good which comes its way. It means Vishakha may desire to enjoy certain specific things. However, Poorvashada simply has the desire to enjoy, and it may enjoy anything.

Looking at a practical example, a Vishakha native may not be able to enjoy a number of beautiful things on the way to his goal. This is because he may be so fixated on his goal that he may simply not be able to notice such things. On the other hand, a Poorvashada native may fix a goal and enjoy all the beautiful things on the way to his goal.

If a Vishakha type tennis player has fixed her eyes on a championship title, she may not be able to fully enjoy, until she has achieved such title. It means, she may not celebrate all her victories, on the way to the title. In the same situation, a Poorvashada type tennis player may not only enjoy each and every victory of hers to the fullest, she may also relax and enjoy in many other possible ways.

Therefore, the list of enjoyable things may be much shorter in case of Vishakha whereas Poorvashada has the ability to enjoy almost everything. Looking at one more example, a

Vishakha native may not care much about taking a walk in a park or sitting on a rooftop in a moonlit night. This is because Vishakha is generally interested in intense physical and sensual types of pleasures only. On the other hand, Poorvashada is a true romantic and it may enjoy a walk, moonlit night and all other things which may be enjoyed. It means Poorvashada goes much wider and much deeper when it comes to enjoy.

Looking at a typical example, a native singing something and dancing along with it at a public place, without caring about what others may think; is very likely to be a Poorvashada native. These natives are capable of creating something to enjoy, if the situation itself doesn't offer anything to enjoy. Hence Poorvashada may be seen as the peak expression of combination of energies of Jupiter and Venus.

Due to this combination of wide variety of characteristics, natives under strong influence of Poorvashada may be found engaging in a wide variety of professions, some of which may seem opposite to each other. For example, one such native may be a religious head and another one may be a fashion model. Likewise, one such native may run a casino and another one may be a spiritual guru. Poorvashada is very good at defying boundaries, whether such boundaries are related to enjoyment or they are related to professional spheres. Even a spiritual guru under strong influence of Poorvashada is likely to be an alive and enjoying type of native; instead of being the silent and serious type.

Poorvashada natives generally have strong will power. Such will power makes them mentally invincible and hence they may not be much bothered by failures and setbacks. Poorvashada natives may be determined to achieve their objectives and goals. Poorvashada natives are generally very patient and they can wait for long periods of time in order to achieve their goals. Due to characteristics like patience, perseverance, optimistic attitude and the ability to remain unshaken during adverse circumstances, they may achieve very good results in many spheres of their lives.

However, if Poorvashada is occupied by unsuitable or malefic planets in a horoscope, characteristics like patience and optimism may turn negative. One such native may keep waiting for very long periods of time in order to achieve his goals, even when there may be little hope left to achieve them. It means the rational and practical chances of achieving such goals may be close to zero. Hence this diehard attitude of Poorvashada natives may at times go against them.

Due to undefeated mental buildup, they may keep sticking to some goals which may have already lost all chances of being achieved. The more difficult part is that Poorvashada natives may not listen to anyone who tells them to quit, as the game may have been over a long time ago. It may be difficult for Poorvashada natives to accept defeat or failure and move on to something else. Therefore, Poorvashada natives may suffer a lot in their lives due to these characteristics. A character who has lost his lover but he is still very positive that he will get her back, despite the fact that she is married, having children and enjoying her family; may very well be a Poorvashada native.

In an extreme case when Poorvashada is occupied by malefic planets and the overall horoscope is also negative in a specific way; one such native may murder the husband of his lover; in the hope that she will come to him after her husband's death. Obsession developed by virtue of strong conviction of winning is one characteristic that makes Poorvashada natives different from other nakshatra type natives. Poorvashada natives may not bear the idea of defeat.

In extreme cases, some of these natives may go insane or even commit suicides when they realize that the goals they pursued for long periods of times are lost. Such Poorvashada natives may take extreme measures to fulfill their goals and they may become dangerous when they get the notion that their goals are slipping away from them. Therefore, Poorvashada is seen as an obsessive, cruel and harsh nakshatra by some Vedic astrologers.

However, such extremes may be witnessed only when Poorvashada is occupied by malefic planets in a horoscope. On the other hand, when Poorvashada is occupied by suitable benefic planets and the overall horoscope is supportive; the native may be wise enough to know, for how long to stick and when to move on.

Poorvashada natives know the art of living and they know how to suck delight out of life. Poorvashada natives are not bothered much by troubles and hurdles that come their way. As a result, they may be capable of enjoying their lives in better ways than many other nakshatra type natives. Poorvashada natives may keep trying to improve their materialistic lives due to influence of Venus on this nakshatra.

They may also be good at showing off their achievements to people around them. Characteristics like outward display of beauty come natural to Poorvashada natives due to strong influence of Venus on this nakshatra. Poorvashada natives may be energetic, creative and expressive. Hence they may achieve success in professional spheres like acting, singing, modelling, sports and other similar fields.

Though Poorvashada displays a number of characteristics, different natives may embrace different characteristics, depending on placements of various planets in this nakshatra, as well as on their overall horoscopes. Looking at planets among navagraha; Sun, Moon, Jupiter, Venus, Mars and Rahu may perform well in Poorvashada. Mercury, Saturn and Ketu may do well in Poorvashada, if the overall horoscope is supportive. Since Poorvashada is loaded with a wide variety of characteristics, almost every planet among navagraha may channelize its energy; when overall horoscope is supportive.

Placements of malefic planets in Poorvashada may weaken or corrupt its characteristics. As a result, the native may suffer from a number of problems, depending on which planets are placed in this nakshatra as well as on his overall horoscope. Taking an example, suppose a malefic combination of Venus and Moon is placed in the first house of a horoscope in Sagittarius, with Moon in Poorvashada and Venus in Moola. Malefic debilitated Saturn is placed in the fifth house in Aries, malefic debilitated Mars is placed in the eighth house in Cancer and the rest of the horoscope is negative in a specific way.

In this case, the native may become obsessed with his lover. Such native may have a long lasting love affair with a woman, such affair may go through many ups and downs and it may finally break. The woman may breakup with the native and she may get married but the native may not let her go out of his mind. The native may keep pursuing her, following her and pressurizing her to get out of her marriage and marry him. In an extreme case when the rest of his horoscope is negative in a specific way, such native may kill his lover. The intention behind such murder may be that if she can't be his, she shouldn't be anyone else's also.

Let's look at performances of various planets in various navamshas of Poorvashada. Starting with Leo navamsha; Jupiter, Sun and Mars may perform very well here whereas Ketu may perform well but not very well in this navamsha.

Ketu is strong in Sagittarius as well as Leo but it doesn't have much comfort in Poorvashada.

Venus may perform above average here whereas Mercury may perform on average or above average here. Venus has great comfort in Poorvashada. Moon may perform on average or above average here; since it has decent strength in Sagittarius as well as Leo, and it is very comfortable in Poorvashada.

Saturn may perform below average here whereas Rahu may perform on average or below average here. Saturn is not strong in Sagittarius, it is weak in Leo and it is not much comfortable in Poorvashada. Rahu is weak in Sagittarius as well as Leo but it is very comfortable in Poorvashada. Among navagraha; Jupiter may be the strongest in this navamsha and Saturn may be the weakest.

Looking at Virgo navamsha; Jupiter, Sun and Mars may perform well or very well here whereas Ketu may perform above average in this navamsha. Ketu is not comfortable in Poorvashada and it is debilitated in Virgo. Moon may perform on average or above average here whereas Mercury may perform above average in this navamsha; since it is exalted in Virgo.

Saturn may perform on average or above average here whereas Rahu may perform above average or well in this navamsha. Saturn is strong in Virgo and Rahu is exalted in this sign. Saturn is not much comfortable in Poorvashada whereas Rahu has great comfort in this nakshatra. Venus may perform on average or below average here; since it is debilitated in Virgo. Among navagraha; Jupiter may be the strongest in this navamsha whereas Venus may be the weakest.

Moving on to Libra navamsha; Jupiter and Mars may perform well or very well here whereas Sun and Ketu may perform well but not very well in this navamsha. Venus may perform well in this navamsha, since it is strong in Libra and it has great comfort in Poorvashada. Moon may perform above average here whereas Mercury may perform on average in this navamsha.

Saturn may perform above average in this navamsha though it may not perform well. Saturn is not strong in Sagittarius and it is not much comfortable in Poorvashada. Rahu may perform above average in this navamsha. Among navagraha; Jupiter may be the strongest in this navamsha. No planet may be significantly weak in this navamsha.

Considering Scorpio navamsha; Jupiter, Sun, Mars and Ketu may perform very well in this navamsha since all of them are strong in Sagittarius as well as Scorpio. Venus may perform above average here whereas Mercury may perform on average in this navamsha; since Venus is stronger than Mercury in Sagittarius and it is more comfortable in Poorvashada than Mercury.

Saturn may perform on average or below average here whereas Rahu may perform below average in this navamsha. Rahu is weak in Sagittarius and it is debilitated in Scorpio. Moon may perform on average in this navamsha. Though it is debilitated in Scorpio; it has decent strength in Sagittarius and it is very comfortable in Poorvashada. Among navagraha; Jupiter may be the strongest in this navamsha whereas Rahu may be the weakest.

Looking at professions, natives under strong influence of Poorvashada may achieve success as actors, singers, musicians, dancers, writers, poets, painters, fashion models, beauticians, sportsmen, sailors, ocean explorers, divers, navy personnel, fishermen, professionals dealing in manufacturing, sales or operations of ships, boats, fairies, yachts and other similar machines; professionals dealing in movie industry, music industry, sports industry, television industry, hotel industry, airline industry, shipping industry, tour and travel industry, luxury vacations, beverage industry, liquor industry, fashion industry, event management industry, logistics industry, ecommerce, information and technology, software industry, real estate, religious places; engineers, doctors, lawyers, teachers, preachers, consultants, religious heads, spiritual heads, astrologers, healers, politicians, government officers and many other types of professionals; depending on their overall horoscopes.

Let's look at some other facts associated with this nakshatra. Poorvashada is considered as a balanced and fierce nakshatra. It is considered as a female nakshatra. Vedic astrology assigns Brahman Varna and air element to Poorvashada. The Gana assigned to Poorvashada is Manava and the Guna assigned to it is Rajasic. It is a downward nakshatra and its Yoni or animal symbol is Monkey.

Uttarashada

Uttarashada is 21st among 27 nakshatras. The first quarter of Uttarashada falls in Sagittarius and the last three quarters of this nakshatra fall in Capricorn.

The literal translation of the word Uttarashada is 'the latter invincible one' or 'the latter undefeated one'. Vedic astrology associates Uttarashada with being invincible like its previous nakshatra Poorvashada. Poorvashada and Uttarashada make a pair like Poorvaphalguni and Uttaraphalguni. They share some characteristics which are similar whereas other characteristics exhibited by them are different.

The main symbol of Uttarashada is taken as the 'the tusk of an elephant'. This symbol sheds light on many characteristics of Uttarashada. The tusk of an elephant is very dear to the elephant. It is considered as the most precious part of an elephant's body. Elephants have been killed since old times to sell their tusks at high prices.

Since the tusk represents great value, this symbol associates great value with Uttarashada. It means natives under strong influence of Uttarashada may gain respect by virtue of being valuable. The symbol of tusk also associates Uttarashada with wars and fights since elephants use their tusks a lot when they fight with one another. The tusks of an elephant have significant value in deciding its control or leadership over other elephants. Hence it adds characteristics like leadership and authority to Uttarashada.

Elephants have been used as symbols of royalty, as only kings or powerful people were able to possess elephants. Mighty kings and powerful people used to show off their power and status by the number of elephants they possessed. Many kings used to ride on elephants whenever they went to battlefields. Elephants also used to make the front rows of the battling crews in order to scare the opposing armies and to inflict maximum damage upon them.

Greater was the number of elephants in an army, stronger the army was considered. Hence Uttarashada is related to characteristics like royalty, status, strength, war and victory through its symbol. Looking at another attribute, elephants are the largest and mightiest animals on land. Elephants are generally calm and friendly in nature. However when provoked or when under threat, they may prove very aggressive, offensive and destructive. It means an elephant can fight and win in most cases, but it generally prefers peace over fight or war.

Elephants are attentive to their surroundings and they keep themselves updated about what is happening around them. Elephants socialize with other animals, they have very good memories and they possess very good amount of aggression. Elephants are social animals and they may go to any lengths to protect their loved ones, especially their young ones. Hence Uttarashada is associated with characteristics like being peaceful, aggressive, destructive, attentive, friendly, social and protective.

Vedic astrology assigns ten Vishvadevas or Universal gods as ruling deities of Uttarashada. Each of these ten Vishvadevas imparts different characteristics to Uttarashada. Vishvadevas are considered as benevolent deities and they possess good characteristics like genuineness, goodness, truthfulness, skillfulness, forgiveness and brightness. Therefore, Uttarashada exhibits all these characteristics due to influences of its ruling deities.

Lord Ganesha is assigned as the final ruling deity of Uttarashada. It is said that Lord Ganesha was once beheaded and he was then revived by fixing an elephant's head on him. Hence he has a lot to do with elephants as well as Uttarashada. Characteristics of Lord Ganesha like being invincible in war, removing all obstacles and working for the wellbeing of the universe are relayed through Uttarashada which make it a much more balanced nakshatra.

Vedic astrology assigns Sun as the planetary ruler of Uttarashada. Characteristics of Sun which are in tune with characteristics of ten Vishvadevas and Lord Ganesha are relayed through Uttarashada. Sun adds characteristics like authority, intelligence, aggression, protection and intelligence to Uttarashada. Influence of Sun provides significant amount of energy to Uttarashada, to conduct its operations. Sun's aggression as well as its ability to wage wars and punish the wrong doers is also relayed through Uttarashada.

These characteristics make Uttarashada an aggressive nakshatra. However, Uttarashada generally shows aggression only when it is required in order to serve higher purposes and not for selfish motives. Contrary to this, Poorvashada may show aggression for selfish motives like when it finds that its goals are slipping away.

Therefore, Uttarashada is considered more controlled compared to Poorvashada. Uttarashada is likely to indulge in the acts of aggression or wars for the benefit of bigger groups of people instead of doing so for selfish motives.

The first quarter of Uttarashada falls in Sagittarius ruled by Jupiter whereas the last three quarters of Uttarashada fall in Capricorn ruled by Saturn. Hence Uttarashada comes under the influence of Jupiter and Saturn also. Since most quarters of Uttarashada lie in Capricorn, the influence of Saturn on Uttarashada is much stronger than influence of Jupiter. Sagittarius exhibits characteristics like intelligence, initiative, faith and optimism. Capricorn exhibits characteristics like patience, practicality, rationality and discipline among other characteristics. All these characteristics are also exhibited through Uttarashada.

The influence of Saturn in particular adds a couple of very important characteristics to Uttarashada, which are the abilities to be rational and practical. If Poorvashada misses something the most, it is these two characteristics. This is because the biggest drawback of Poorvashada is to get fixed on its goals and keep chasing them, even when they may not be rational or realistic any longer. This tendency may lead Poorvashada natives to obsessive behavior patterns. Hence they may get stuck or they may engage in unhealthy measures to achieve their goals.

Characteristics like rationality and practicality may help Uttarashada natives decide when to pursue goals and when to leave them. Hence Uttarashada may not keep following its goals unrealistically like Poorvashada. Uttarashada may be rational enough to know when a goal has lost its relevance, and it moves on in such case. Characteristic of practicality may help Uttarashada natives when something is not practical. Hence they may not pursue it or fantasize about it; like Poorvashada natives.

Taking an example, if the lover of a Poorvashada native breaks up with him, she gets married and she has children, the native may still keep pursuing her. Such Poorvashada native may convince or pressurize her to walk out of her marriage which may be happy or very happy; in order to be with him. This is neither rational nor practical.

On the other hand, an Uttarashada native in the same situation may not do any of these things. Though he may love his lover a lot, he may move on the moment she gets married. He may still love her but he may do nothing to pursue her, follow her, pressurize her or trouble her. He may understand that such acts are not rational and practical; and he may stay away from them.

Considering another probability, even if such lover contacts such Uttarashada native to have an extramarital affair with him, while she is married and having children, the native may refuse. Such Uttarashada native may be wise enough to know that such an affair may only end up causing problems. Hence he may choose to stay away from it, even if he loves the woman a lot.

Let's suppose, the marriage of this woman fails and she gets divorced. If she now gets in touch with such Uttarashada native, he may reinitiate the relationship, if his circumstances allow. If the horoscope is supportive, he may marry her and assume responsibility of her children, being completely rational and practical.

Hence Uttarashada is a practical and realistic nakshatra and it may not fall victim to unrealistic hopes, convictions and obsessions like the previous nakshatra Poorvashada. Uttarashada natives may be goal oriented and they may also have good amounts of patience to wait for fruits of their efforts. However, they may be able to quit chasing such goals when they realize that such goals have lost their relevance or they are not practical any longer.

In the recent example, though the lover may still be relevant to Uttarashada native after her marriage, it may not be rational and practical to get her engaged in an extramarital affair. Looking at relevance, such Uttarashada native may himself break up with his lover if he realizes that they don't work well as a couple. Hence the whole concept of being with this woman loses its relevance and such Uttarashada native may walk out of such relationship.

Due to these characteristics, the obsessive streak seen in case of Poorvashada natives reduces significantly in case of Uttarashada natives. As a result, Uttarashada natives may be in better control of themselves. Accordingly, they may have the ability to leave things when they feel that attending to them any longer is waste of time and effort.

Uttarashada natives may be disciplined in their actions due to influence of Saturn and Capricorn on this nakshatra. At times, Uttarashada natives may be rigid and harsh by virtue of being over disciplined due to influence of Saturn on Uttarashada. This may especially be the case when Saturn is placed in Capricorn in Uttarashada; and that too in the first house of a horoscope.

In such case, influence of Saturn may become too strong on Uttarashada as well as on the native. As already mentioned, the first house of a horoscope is the core of it. Hence the energy of any planet, sign or nakshatra; registered in this house tends to work as dominant energy; influencing the entire personality of the native.

Uttarashada natives generally have good respect for traditions. Hence they may follow traditions set by their ancestors and society; in most cases. Ancestors are also considered to be among ten Vishvadevas who are considered as the ruling deities of Uttarashada. Due to influence of ancestors, Uttarashada natives may respect their traditional values. Hence they may not like people who go against such traditions or traditional values and some of these natives may take harsh actions against the people breaking these traditions.

Since Uttarashada has good sense of separating right from wrong, Uttarashada natives may get offended only when good traditions are violated. Uttarashada natives may have the ability to change or break traditions when they feel that such traditions may not be useful any longer or they may be harmful. Such characteristic of Uttarashada natives may help them gain respect and status in society. The tendency to change/break traditions may be much higher in Sagittarius part of this nakshatra. Capricorn part of this nakshatra may prefer sticking to traditions, more than changing them.

Though Uttarashada natives may also have tendency to engage in fights or wars like Poorvashada natives, Uttarashada natives may be much wiser in making such decisions. They may engage in such actions when they are required for benefits of bigger groups of people, or they may do so for self-defense. It means a head of state under strong influence of Uttarashada may not initiate war against another country for selfish motives.

However, he may be capable enough to engage in war and protect his country, if any country attacks. This is a war fought for self-defense. Looking at another probability, if a country attacks another country which is an ally of this native's country, such Uttarashada native may engage in war. He may do so to protect the ally as well as to restore balance in the region.

Contrary to this, Poorvashada natives may engage in acts of war to fulfill their obsessions or to achieve their unrealistic goals. Uttarashada natives may engage in acts like war, only to restore peace and balance; and they may not do so for selfish motives. It means a head of state under strong influence of Uttarashada may not attack another country to gain some territory or for other benefits.

Uttarashada natives may also be good at forgiving even their enemies when the final objective is achieved. They may feel that hurting or harming anyone at that time may not be necessary. It means a head of state under strong influence of Uttarashada may not commit violence against the enemy who has been defeated or who has surrendered. The final objective of this native may be to restore balance. Hence whenever such balance is restored, he may stop war. It means deep down; Uttarashada natives may be peace loving and they may choose war only when there is no other genuine option left.

Uttarashada natives may be skilled at engaging in wars as well as in winning wars. It means such natives may go to wars, duly prepared for long term implications of wars; as well as after assessing strengths and weaknesses of their enemies. Uttarashada has the highest rate of winning wars among all 27 nakshatras, which tells how gifted Uttarashada natives may be at winning wars. The beauty of Uttarashada is that despite being able to win in most cases, it may not like wars and it rather likes peace and balance.

This characteristic resembles with that exhibited by an elephant. An elephant may prove to be most dangerous and destructive enemy among land animals. However, an elephant still loves peace and it engages in war only when necessary. These characteristics make Uttarashada more balanced compared to a number of other nakshatras. Hence Uttarashada natives may be gifted with bigger visions, working in accordance with universal theme.

It should be noted that these tendencies may hold true, only when suitable benefic planets are placed in this nakshatra. On the other hand, malefic planets placed in this nakshatra may distort/misuse its characteristics. Hence the skills given by Uttarashada may be used to create destructive results. One such native may become a terrorist and he may kill many people for selfish motives. If one such native becomes the head of a state; he may wage wars on many countries; for selfish motives.

Uttarashada natives may be more focused on their professions, compared to their relationships. As a result, they may achieve a lot through their professions when their overall horoscopes are supportive. However, they may not witness the same good results in relationships like marriage. Uttarashada may not prove very bad for marriage unless malefic planets misuse its energy.

However, it may still cause problems in this sphere. Hence Uttarashada natives may face problems in their marriages; primarily because they may not be able to give sufficient time to their life partners, as they may be too busy taking care of their professions. This tendency may be significantly reduced in Sagittarius part of Uttarashada whereas it may be duly effective in Capricorn part of this nakshatra.

Uttarashada exhibits a wide variety of characteristics. However, different natives may embrace different characteristics, depending on placements of various planets in this nakshatra, as well as on their overall horoscopes. Looking at planets among navagraha; Sun, Jupiter and Ketu may perform better in Sagittarius part of this nakshatra. Moon, Venus, Mercury, Saturn and Rahu may perform better in Capricorn part of this nakshatra. Mars may perform well in Sagittarius as well as Capricorn part of this nakshatra;

though it may have advantage in Capricorn part. Placements of malefic planets in Uttarashada may weaken or corrupt its characteristics. As a result, the native may suffer from various types of problems, depending on his overall horoscope.

Let's look at performances of various planets in various navamshas of Uttarashada. Starting with Sagittarius navamsha; Jupiter, Sun, Mars and Ketu may perform very well here; since all of them are strong in Sagittarius and they are very comfortable in Uttarashada. Jupiter may be comfortable but not very comfortable in Uttarashada.

Saturn may perform on average here whereas Mercury may perform on average or below average in this navamsha. Both Saturn and Mercury are not strong in Sagittarius. Venus may perform on average in this navamsha, since it is stronger than Mercury and Saturn in Sagittarius. Rahu may perform below average or poorly in this navamsha since it is weak in Sagittarius. Moon may perform on average in this navamsha. Among navagraha; Jupiter may be the strongest in this navamsha whereas Rahu may be the weakest.

Looking at Capricorn navamsha; Venus, Mercury and Rahu may perform well or very well in this navamsha; since they are all strong in Capricorn. Saturn and Mars may perform very well here, since Saturn is very strong in Capricorn and Mars is exalted in this sign. Apart from that, both of them are very comfortable in Uttarashada. Sun may perform above average here; since it has decent strength in Capricorn and it is very comfortable in Uttarashada.

Moon may perform on average here whereas Ketu may perform on average or above average in this navamsha. Jupiter may perform very poorly in this navamsha. Among all 108 navamshas of 27 nakshatras; Jupiter may be the weakest in this navamsha. Among navagraha; Mars and Saturn may be the strongest in this navamsha whereas Jupiter may be the weakest.

Moving on to Aquarius navamsha; Saturn and Mars may perform very well here whereas Mercury, Rahu and Venus may perform well or very well here. Mercury, Rahu and Venus are not as strong in Capricorn as Saturn and Mars. Sun may perform on average here; since it has decent strength in Capricorn and it is very comfortable in Uttarashada but it is weak in Aquarius.

Moon may perform below average here; since it is not comfortable in Aquarius. Ketu may perform on average in this navamsha whereas Jupiter may perform poorly in this navamsha. Among navagraha; Saturn may be the strongest in this navamsha whereas Jupiter may be the weakest.

Considering Pisces navamsha; Mars, Venus and Saturn may perform well or very well here. Mars and Saturn are not strong in Pisces whereas Venus is exalted in Pisces but it is not as strong in Capricorn as Saturn and Mars. Mercury and Rahu may perform on average or above average in this navamsha; since both of them are debilitated in Pisces.

Moon may perform above average in this navamsha; since it has decent strength in Capricorn and it is strong in Pisces. Ketu may perform well in this navamsha; since it has decent strength in Capricorn, it is exalted in Pisces and it is very comfortable in Uttarashada. Jupiter may perform below average or on average in this navamsha since it is strong in Pisces. Among navagraha; Venus may be the strongest in this navamsha. No planet may be significantly weak in this navamsha.

Looking at professions, natives under strong influence of Uttarashada may practice as wrestlers, athletes, sword fighters, boxers, karate fighters and other types of combat sportsmen,

sportsmen in general, police officers, army officers, naval officers, air force officers, defense ministers, home ministers, prime ministers, presidents, government officers, defense contractors, lawyers, judges, doctors, engineers, software developers, consultants, astrologers, advisors, psychologists, teachers, preachers, religious heads, spiritual heads, religious gurus, spiritual gurus, professionals dealing in industries related to defense, real estate industry, sports equipment, legal services, event management industry, media industry, transport industry, movie industry and many other types of professionals, depending on their overall horoscopes.

Let's look at some other facts associated with this nakshatra. Uttarashada is considered as a balanced and fixed nakshatra. It is considered as a female nakshatra. Vedic astrology assigns Kshatriya Varna and air element to Uttarashada. The Gana assigned to Uttarashada is Manava and the Guna assigned to it is Sattwic. It is an upward nakshatra and its Yoni or animal symbol is Mongoose.

Shravana

Shravana is 22nd among 27 nakshatras. All four quarters of Shravana fall in Capricorn. Shravana is ruled by Lord Narayana, one of the three supreme Gods. Hence it becomes an important nakshatra.

Out of 27 nakshatras, only three nakshatras are ruled by trinity. Rohini is ruled by Lord Brahma, Ardra is ruled by Lord Shiva in his Rudra form and Shravana is ruled by Lord Narayana. Hence these three nakshatras are considered special in their own ways.

The literal translation of the word Shravana is 'the ability to hear' or 'the process of hearing'. An alternate meaning is also associated with this word which translates into 'the limping one'. According to Vedic astrology, both these meanings have a lot to do in deciding the characteristics of Shravana. Shravana is associated with more than one symbol. A sequence of three uneven footsteps is taken as a symbol of Shravana. These are considered to be the three steps taken by Lord Narayana during one of his incarnations known as Vaaman Avatar.

Once upon a time, there was a powerful demon king Bali who conquered the three worlds known as Prithvi (earth), Swarg (heaven) and Paataal Loka (the underworld). Indra the ruler of heaven requested Lord Narayana to put end to

Bali's misdeeds. Lord Narayana incarnated on earth as a dwarf Brahman. Accordingly, this Avatar of Lord Narayana is known as Vaaman Avatar in Indian mythology, where Vaaman means dwarf.

Bali was known as a person true to his word and Lord Narayana decided to take advantage of this good characteristic of Bali. The demon king was getting a Yagya performed. One of the rituals demanded that upon completion of Yagya, Bali should offer donations to Brahmans. Upon completion of Yagya, Bali asked Brahmans what they wanted as offerings. Vaaman stood up and asked for land which could be measured with three steps.

Bali made promise to grant Vaaman's wish. Hearing this, Vaaman grew so big that his head vanished in the sky. He measured earth and the underworld in the first step and he measured heaven in the second step. Vaaman asked Bali as to what he should claim with his third step since he had already claimed everything Bali had, with his first two steps. To keep his word, Bali bowed before Vaaman and asked him to claim his head with the third step; as it was the only thing left in his possession. Vaaman blessed Bali for making donation to the Lord himself. He then sent Bali to another world.

This incident is very meaningful. It indicates the cleverness of Lord Narayana, which enabled him to get his job done without any violence. This clever and tricky side of Lord Narayana is relayed through Shravana. Accordingly, natives under strong influence of Shravana are considered among the cleverest type of natives. Whether this characteristic of cleverness exhibited by Shravna is used positively or negatively; depends on the overall horoscope of the native under consideration.

In order to get his wish granted, Lord Narayana had to ask for donation. The Lord, who is supposed to give only, had to ask. This shows the determination and dedication of Lord Narayana, as he was willing to go to any lengths in order to get his job done. Hence characteristics like determination, dedication and flexibility are relayed through Shravana. In fact, Shravna is considered as one of the most determined and fixed nakshatra. It means once it sets a goal, it may go to any lengths in order to achieve such goal.

It should be noted that Shravana represents non-violent and clever side of Lord Narayana. Hence Shravana natives may not engage in direct physical violence to achieve their goals, unlike the natives belonging to some other nakshatras. Shravana natives may achieve their goals with the help of characteristics like cleverness, skillfulness, flexibility, diplomacy, determination and dedication.

Hence even if a native is under strong malefic influence of Shravana and he wishes to work for selfish motives, he may not directly engage in violence. Such Shravana native may find diplomatic ways of getting his job done. For this reason, most criminals under strong malefic influence of Shravana are likely to be white collar criminals. Apart from that, Shravana type criminals are more likely to engage in financial crimes, scams and other such crimes, which generally do not involve the element of violence.

Most such crimes are committed through tricks, cleverness and skills. Hence placements of malefic planets in Shravana may produce some of the best con artists, master thieves, professionals dealing in financial crimes like fake currency, smuggling of various items and other such crimes. It means a master thief who steals a piece of art or another valuable item from a highly secured place, with perfect planning and leaving no trace; may very well be a Shravana type native. As mentioned many times, any energy can be used positively or negatively; and it has no wish of its own.

Looking at the Vaaman incident, Bali was deceived because he underestimated Vaaman. He might have thought how much land a Vaaman could measure with three steps. It means there is often much more to Shravana than meets the eye. Hence natives under strong influence of Shravana may hold much more wealth, power, skill or knowledge than they seem to possess. It means one should not underestimate a native under strong influence of Shravana since he may hold many secret weapons.

Criminal heads under strong influence of Shravana may often have hidden connections with government officers and politicians. They may not disclose such connections and they may use these connections to kill the competition as well as to stay protected.

Looking at this fact from another angle, government officers under strong influence of Shravana may have strong and hidden connections with people in high places. Such officers may use these connections to stay protected as well as to stay ahead in the competition. Whatever field Shravana natives may engage in, they may hold much more power or resources, than they may seem to hold.

A symbol of 'ear' is also associated with this nakshatra. This symbol renders many characteristics to Shravana. An ear represents the ability to hear and accordingly the ability to learn and preserve. It should be noted that in ancient times, knowledge was transferred by means of oral teaching, which means through ears. Students listened to their teachers or gurus carefully and they preserved what they heard. Therefore, Shravana is directly related to the ability to learn and preserve.

Vedic astrology assigns Lord Narayana as the ruling deity of Shravana. Much has already been mentioned about influence of Lord Narayana on Shravana. Characteristics of Lord Narayana like cleverness, organizing skills, determination, dedication, flexibility, patience, perseverance, diplomacy and communication skills are relayed through Shravana. These characteristics make Shravana one of the most organized and cleverest among 27 nakshatras.

Vedic astrology also assigns goddess Saraswati as the ruling deity of Shravana. The influence of goddess Saraswati adds characteristics like the ability to gain knowledge, good listening abilities, good speech abilities and good sense of music and other arts, to Shravana.

Vedic astrology assigns Moon as the planetary ruler of Shravana. Influence of Moon brings characteristics like gentleness, receptiveness and the ability to connect to masses and influence them, to Shravana. All four quarters of Shravana fall in Capricorn ruled by Saturn. The Influences of Saturn and Capricorn add characteristics like organizational skills, management skills, administrative skills, analytical ability, discipline, patience, practicality and perseverance to Shravana. As a result, Shravana natives may achieve success through a wide variety of professional spheres.

Shravana natives are generally very patient and persevering. They may keep moving towards their goals until they achieve them. Since Shravana natives may be clever and practical, they may not fall for unrealistic goals unlike some other nakshatra type natives. Shravana is a persevering nakshatra and natives under strong influence of this nakshatra may try their best to reach their goals.

Shravana natives may be good at gaining knowledge and then applying such knowledge to produce results. Shravana natives are generally social in nature and they may have good networks of friends and colleagues. Such networks may be used by Shravana natives in various organizational activities in order to achieve bigger goals. Shravana natives may be good at influencing and charming people and then using them to get benefits from them or through them.

Shravana natives may be good listeners and they may also be good speakers. Which one of these sides may be dominant in one such native, depends on placements of various planets in this nakshatra, as well as on his overall horoscope. Taking an example, if benefic Saturn is placed in the first or second house of a horoscope in Capricorn in Shravana, the native may listen more or much more than he may speak. The combination of Saturn with Shravana may put more focus on listening and preserving than on speaking and preaching.

Taking another example, if Mercury is placed in the second house of a horoscope in Capricorn in Shravana, the native may speak more than he may listen. Mercury is the general signifier of speech and the second house represents speech among other things. Hence such combination of Mercury with Shravna may put more focus on speaking, though the native may have his fair share of listening also. One such native may engage in a profession where verbal abilities may be valued a lot. This is because Mercury rules the tenth house in this horoscope; since Virgo falls in the tenth house. Hence the native may use his verbal abilities along with other abilities to achieve success in profession.

Shravana exhibits a number of characteristics. However, different natives may embrace different characteristics, depending on placements of various planets in this nakshatra, as well as depending on their overall horoscopes. Looking at planets among navagraha; Moon, Venus, Mars, Mercury, Saturn, Rahu and Ketu may perform well in Shravana. Sun may perform well in Shravana, when supported by overall horoscope. Jupiter may not be much comfortable with the energy of Shravana.

Though most planets among navagraha may channelize the energy of Shravana, they may produce different effects. Placement of benefic Moon in the first house of a horoscope in Capricorn in Shravana may bless the native with a post of authority in government or in a private organization; depending on his overall horoscope. The native under strong influence of such Moon in Shravana may also achieve success as a professional dealing in telecom sector, real estate sector, event management industry, legal sector, entertainment industry, hospitality industry; and some other types of professional, depending on the rest of his horoscope.

Placement of benefic Mars in the first house of a horoscope in Capricorn in Shravana forms Ruchaka Yoga in the horoscope. The native under strong influence of such Ruchaka Yoga in Shravana may achieve authority in government as an officer or as a politician. Formation of Ruchaka Yoga in a horoscope is generally considered to bless the native with success in defence services. However in this case, such Ruchaka Yoga may bend the native towards administrative services, revenue services, telecommunication, broadcast and other such services.

This is because Ruchaka Yoga formed in Shravana may not favour engagement in direct physical aggression of extreme types. Such Ruchaka Yoga may instead make the native interested in professional spheres represented by Shravana. However, the native may serve for defense services in different ways. For example, such native having Ruchaka Yoga in Shravana may become an administrative officer and later in his career, he may serve as defence secretary.

This type of Ruchaka Yoga may also bless the native with power and authority through politics. In such case, the native may become home minister, finance minister, telecom minister or the minster for commerce. Such Ruchaka Yoga in Shravana may also bless the native through various types of sports; though the native may not engage in extreme physical sports like boxing and wrestling.

Looking at another variation, if benefic Saturn is placed in the first house of a horoscope in Capricorn in Shravana, Shasha Yoga is formed. The native under strong influence of such Shasha Yoga in Shravana may achieve success through financial sector, real estate sector, telecom sector, frozen food industry or education sector. This type of Shasha Yoga may also bless the native with authority in the house of government through job or through politics, depending on his overall horoscope.

If the native achieves authority as an officer, he may become an administrative officer, a revenue officer or a judge. If such Shasha Yoga blesses him with authority through politics, the native may serve as telecom minister, finance minister, information and broadcast minister or education minister. If the overall horoscope is strong, such Sasha Yoga in Shravana may bless the native with the post of chief minister, governor, prime minster or president. In case the native becomes a judge, such Shasha Yoga may bless him with the post of chief justice of Supreme Court or Apex court; when supported by his overall horoscope.

Placements of malefic planets in Shravana may weaken or corrupt its characteristics. As a result, the native may suffer from a wide variety of problems, depending on his overall horoscope. Some natives under strong influence of malefic planets in Shravana may engage in various types of crimes. Since Shravana is good at the art of disguise, it may become very difficult to deal with such criminals.

Most criminals under strong malefic influence of Shravana may be white collar criminals. Such natives may be shrewd and they may successfully run their illegal businesses for many years without getting caught or without even getting recognized as criminals. It means for many years, they may not have any criminal records and they may keep operating under the radar.

Let's look at performances of various planets in various navamshas of Shravana. Starting with Aries navamsha; Mars may perform very well in this navamsha; since it is exalted in Capricorn and it is strong in Aries. Saturn, Mercury, Venus and Rahu may perform well but not very well here. Saturn is debilitated in Aries whereas Venus, Mercury and Rahu are not as strong in Capricorn as Saturn and Mars. Apart from that, they are not strong in Aries.

Moon may perform on overage or above average here; since it has decent strength in Capricorn as well as Aries; and it is very comfortable in Shravana. Sun may perform above average here whereas Ketu may perform on average or above average in this navamsha. Jupiter may perform below average or on average but not poorly in this navamsha, since it is strong in Aries. Among navagraha; Mars may be the strongest in this navamsha. No planet may be significantly weak in this navamsha.

Looking at Taurus navamsha; Mars, Venus, Rahu and Saturn may perform very well in this navamsha whereas Mercury may perform well or very well here. Saturn may do its best work in this navamsha; among all 4 navamshas of Shravana. Rahu is exalted in Taurus and within the sign of Capricorn; it may deliver second best results in this navamsha. Rahu may produce best results in Virgo navamsha of Dhanishtha; within the sign of Capricorn. Though Rahu is exalted in Taurus as well as Virgo navamsha; it is more comfortable in Dhanishtha.

Moon may perform well in this navamsha; since it has decent strength in Capricorn, it is exalted in Taurus and it is very comfortable in Shravana. Within Capricorn; Moon may deliver its best performance in this navamsha. Sun may perform on average here; since it is not strong in Capricorn as well as Taurus. Ketu may perform below average in this navamsha since it is debilitated in Taurus and not strong in Capricorn. Jupiter may perform poorly in this navamsha. Among navagraha; Saturn may be the strongest in this navamsha whereas Jupiter may be the weakest.

Moving on to Gemini navamsha; Mars, Venus, Mercury, Saturn and Rahu may perform well or very well here. Mercury is not as strong as Saturn and Mars in Capricorn but is stronger than them in Gemini and it is very comfortable in Shravana. Moon may perform above average here; since it is not strong in Capricorn as well as Gemini but it is very comfortable in Shravana.

Sun may perform on average or below average here whereas Ketu may perform below average in this navamsha. Sun is not strong in Gemini though it has decent strength in this sign whereas Ketu is weak in Gemini. Jupiter may perform poorly in this navamsha; since it is debilitated in Capricorn and it doesn't have much strength in Gemini. Among navagraha; Saturn may be the strongest in this navamsha whereas Jupiter may be the weakest.

Considering Cancer navamsha; Saturn may perform well or very well in this navamsha whereas Venus may perform well here. Rahu and Mercury may perform above average or well in this navamsha. Mercury is weak in Cancer but it is very comfortable in Shravana and it is strong in Capricorn. Rahu is not strong in Cancer but it is also very comfortable in Shravna. Mars may perform well but not very well in this navamsha, since it is debilitated in Cancer.

Moon may perform above average or well in this navamsha; since it is strong in Cancer. Sun may perform below average in this navamsha; since it has decent strength in Capricorn and it is weak in Cancer. Ketu may perform on average here and Jupiter may also perform on average but not above average in this navamsha. Though Jupiter is exalted in Cancer, it is debilitated in Capricorn and it is not much comfortable in Shravana. Among navagraha; Saturn may be the strongest in this navamsha. No planet may be significantly weak in this navamsha.

Looking at professions, natives under strong influence of Shravana may practice as teachers, preachers, consultants, advisors, psychiatrists, astrologers, psychics, healers, religious gurus, spiritual gurus, actors, writers, singers, musicians, dancers, producers, directors, sportsmen, doctors, engineers, software developers, bankers, financial analysts, stock market professionals, researchers, explorers, professionals dealing in education sector, financial sector, real estate sector, telecom sector, media industry, movie industry, music industry, hotel industry, tour and travel industry, software industry, hearing aids making industry, television industry, radio industry, frozen food industry, automobile industry, airline industry, medical equipment industry and many other types of professionals, depending on their overall horoscopes.

Let's look at some other facts associated with this nakshatra. Shravana is considered as a passive and movable nakshatra. It is considered as a male nakshatra. Vedic astrology assigns Shudra Varna and air element to Shravana. The Gana assigned to Shravana is Deva and the Guna assigned to it is Rajasic. It is an upward nakshatra and its Yoni or animal symbol is Monkey.

Dhanishtha

Dhanishtha is 23rd among 27 nakshatras. The first two quarters of Dhanishtha fall in Capricorn and the last two quarters of this nakshatra fall in Aquarius.

The literal meaning of the word Dhanishtha is 'the wealthiest one'. Vedic astrology translates the meaning of Dhanishtha as wealthy and beneficent. Strong benefic influence of Dhanishtha in a horoscope is capable of blessing the native with wealth and status. Natives under strong influence of Dhanishtha may also enjoy various types of pleasures in their lives.

A musical drum is taken as the main symbol of Dhanishtha. This symbol associates Dhanishtha with all types of musical activities. Accordingly, Dhanishtha natives may be inclined towards one form of music or another. It is believed by some that the musical drum used as the symbol of Dhanishtha is the Damaru of Lord Shiva. Some others believe it is a drum which is hollow from inside. A Damaru is also hollow from inside and it creates music from hollowness.

This indicates the characteristic of creating things out of nothing. It means natives under strong influence of Dhanishtha may bring beautiful creations to life, virtually out of nothing. It also means that Dhanishtha natives may create success, money and wealth out of nothing. Hence Dhanishtha natives may achieve success and wealth, even if they are born in poor families.

A Flute is also considered as a symbol of Dhanishtha. The symbol of Flute again relates Dhanishtha to music and creation of something out of nothing. Hence Dhanishtha natives may be creative and they may create wealth, money, success, music and other pieces of creation out of nothing.

Since old times, drums have been used to convey messages to masses of people. Whenever kings needed to make public announcements, drums were used to gather crowds. It is believed that through the sound of Damaru, Lord Shiva also sends messages to all creatures or to some specific creatures in the zone. Therefore, Dhanishtha represents characteristics of connecting to masses and communicating with them.

Due to characteristics like creativity and the ability to connect to masses; Dhanishtha may bless natives under its strong influence with success through various creative fields. Hence Dhanishtha natives may achieve success as various types of artists who play musical instruments like flute, drum, guitar, violin, piano and all other such instruments. Dhanishtha may also bless the natives with success through other creative fields and they may become actors, singers, dancers, writers and other types of creative artists. Dhanishtha as a nakshatra has a lot to do with creativity of all types.

Vedic astrology assigns eight Vasus as the ruling deities of Dhanishtha. Vasus are a particular group of gods. Other groups are Rudras and Adityas. The eight Vasus are known as Apah, Dhruva, Dhara, Anila, Soma, Anala, Pratyush and Prabhasa. Each one of these Vasus adds his unique characteristics to Dhanishtha. Hence Dhanishtha is blessed with characteristics like musical abilities, confidence, organizational skills, being full of energy, being fixed in nature, reliability, charitable nature, resourcefulness, business skills, discrimination, joyfulness, hopefulness, goodness, sensitivity, excellence, wealth, safety and many other good characteristics possessed by these eight Vasus.

Lord Shiva is assigned as the final presiding deity of Dhanishtha. Accordingly, some characteristics of Lord Shiva like his musical abilities and his dancing abilities are relayed through Dhanishtha. Lord Shiva is considered as the lord of dances in his Nataraja form. Among various types of dances he engages in; two forms of Tandava hold special significance.

Lord Shiva uses Ananda Tandava to promote creation, joy and happiness. On the other hand, he uses Rudra Tandava to cause destruction. In the deepest sense, Rudra Tandava represents the act of getting rid of such characteristics within you, which may hinder your growth like anger, depression, frustration and sorrows. Once it is done, Ananda Tandava is used to express the state of being joyful and blissful.

Hence Lord Shiva exhibits two seemingly opposite sides of his personality through these two forms of Tandava. In reality, they are not opposite and they are complementary, since one can't survive without the other. In the deepest sense, creation can't be complete on its own and it always needs destruction to complement it. Let's look at this aspect with the help of some examples from different spheres.

Eating food is a creative activity since it helps the body achieve growth, stay healthy and gain energy to perform daily routines. However, the act of eating or drinking is not complete without the act of excretion, which is a destructive act. Through the acts of excretion like sweating, urinating and defecating; we destroy. However, this destruction is only meant to make us better by getting rid of unwanted parts of food. Imagine what may happen if we only eat and drink; and there is no excretion?

Trees grow or create leaves and then they destroy or shed them. However, such destruction only means well for them as they will soon have new leaves. Imagine what may happen if trees keep holding onto their dry and unwanted leaves. The birth of a baby is considered as the peak of creativity. However, this too is accompanied by destruction as this baby will die one day. It looks like a bad thing but imagine what may happen if people are only born and no one dies.

It may simply become impossible to sustain the system with such huge number of people living at the same time. Imagine you are five thousand years old and you witness two hundred generations born after you. Even if you don't age and you stay young, the world around you may be nothing less than chaos. How are you going to handle thousands of family members and all other complications associated with immortality? Apart from that, life is meaningful only if death is there.

We feel the need to study, enjoy our youths, engage in professions, get married, have children and grow wiser, only because life comes with expiry date. All these attributes may get lost or corrupted if we become immortals. Hence destruction of life is necessary for creation of life. It means they are complementary and not opposite.

Let's look at the final example now. In the deepest sense, we only destroy so that we may be able to create. On account of various events and activities; elements like anger, frustration, sadness and other such elements may build inside us. With time, they may get stronger and it may become difficult for us to handle them and to live with them. Hence we engage in acts of aggression which in reality are acts of destruction.

These acts are meant to destroy excessive buildups of anger, frustration and other such elements. Once they are destroyed, we feel relieved and capable of enjoying. Through our daily routines, they build up again and the need to destroy them rises again. Hence the outburst of troublesome emotions is the act through which we destroy what is disturbing us; so that we may be able to create again; which means to grow and to enjoy life again.

Therefore, two opposite looking forms of Tandava practiced by Lord Shiva in reality are complementary to each other. Dhanishtha also represents both these sides of Lord Shiva. It means Dhanishtha represents creative as well as destructive characteristics of Lord Shiva. In other words, Dhanishtha exhibits characteristics belonging to soft form of Lord Shiva as well as those belonging to aggressive form of Lord Shiva.

This makes Dhanishtha more versatile compared to Ardra and Shravana. Ardra primarily represents aggressive form of Lord Shiva and Shravana features non-aggressive side of Lord Narayana. Both Ardra and Shravana seem incomplete in the sense that they represent one side of these lords and they lack the opposite or complementary sides.

When it comes to Dhanishtha, it is complete in the sense that it represents both sides of Lord Shiva's personality. It should be noted that Ardra and Shravana represent much broader spectrums of personalities of Lord Shiva and Lord Narayana, respectively. Dhanishtha on the other hand, primarily represents the creative and destructive aspect of Lord Shiva's personality.

Hence Dhanishtha is not as versatile as the other two nakshatras when it comes to represent different aspects of personalities of their respective lords. However, it is better in the sense that it gives a complete picture of one aspect of Lord Shiva. This aspect is the aspect of creation and destruction, to be seen as two sides of the same coin. Hence the coin is complete, only when both sides are present. Due to representation of both aspects of this characteristic of Lord Shiva; Dhanishtha may be creative as well as destructive.

Vedic astrology assigns Mars as the ruling planet of Dhanishtha. Hence Dhanishtha gets characteristics like bravery, courage, energy, aggression, initiative and warrior abilities from Mars. The first two quarters of Dhanishtha fall in Capricorn ruled by Saturn and the last two quarters of Dhanishtha fall in Aquarius, also ruled by Saturn. Saturn is known to exhibit characteristics like administrative abilities, organizational abilities, perseverance and discipline among other characteristics. These characteristics of Saturn are exhibited through Dhanishtha, making it a goal oriented nakshatra. Dhanishtha natives are generally very good at pursuing their goals until they achieve them.

Since Mars is exalted in Capricorn and it rules Dhanishtha, quarters of this nakshatra falling in this sign may receive too much energy at times. Accordingly, natives under strong influence of Capricorn part of Dhanishtha may be more aggressive and energetic than those under strong influence of Aquarius part of Dhanishtha. This extra energy provided by Dhanishtha in Capricorn part may prove good or bad for a native, depending on how the native is able to channelize it. Due to this extra energy, natives under strong influence of Capricorn part of Dhanishtha may often be seen engaging in sports, defence services and other such activities which are creative or destructive and which at the same time; require a lot of energy.

In comparison, the Aquarius part of Dhanishtha is softer and easier to channelize. As a result, it tends to channelize its energy in relatively softer ways. It may be assumed that Capricorn part of Dhanishtha represents Rudra Tandava which means destructive aspect, more than creative aspect. However, Aquarius part of Dhanishtha represents Ananda Tandava which means creative aspect, more than destructive aspect. As a result, natives under strong influence of Aquarius part of Dhanishtha may be more inclined to work as actors, musicians, singers, writers, dancers, painters and many other types of creative professionals.

Since Capricorn part of Dhanishtha is more aggressive, it is difficult to handle. Hence placement of exalted Mars in this part of Dhanishtha may cause problems in the sphere of relationships, especially the relationships like lover affair and marriage. For this reason, Manglik Dosh formed by malefic Mars in Capricorn part of Dhanishtha may prove much more troublesome than Manglik Dosh formed by malefic Mars in Aquarius part of Dhanishtha. Even the placement of benefic Mars in Capricorn part of Dhanishtha in relevant houses of a horoscope may cause problems in marriage; though such problems may be manageable.

Dhanishtha natives may have good interest in music and some of them may choose professions related to music. Dhanishtha natives may have good amount of confidence and bravery due to influence of Mars on this nakshatra. These characteristics may become stronger in Capricorn part of Dhanishtha. Hence a number of natives under strong influence of Capricorn part of Dhanishtha may be seen practicing in the fields like army, police, sports and other such fields.

Dhanishtha natives are generally fixed in nature and they work hard to reach their goals. Due to characteristics like perseverance, confidence and good organizational abilities possessed by them, these natives may be able to achieve their goals in most cases. Dhanishtha natives may have good sense of business, trade and diplomacy. They may use these characteristics to climb the ladders of success in their lives.

Dhanishtha natives may be good at enjoying their lives and whatever they achieve in their lives. Therefore, these natives are generally seen living happily. In fact, living happy and prosperous lives is one of the main characteristics possessed by Dhanishtha natives. These natives may be good at giving outward expressions to troublesome emotions like anger or sadness. Hence they may let them out every now and then. Though such acts of these natives may look troublesome, these acts may end up refreshing them and reviving them.

As a result, they may be able to enjoy more and create more; since they are able to destroy more of their troublesome emotions. Due to this characteristic, natives under strong influence of Dhanishtha may also do well as actors since they may be gifted with the art of finding outward expressions for emotions. Here also, they may be especially good at expressing anger, sadness and joy; since these are some of the most intense types of emotions. When it comes to romance and love, the emotions engaged are relatively softer, unless there is a touch of tragedy or vengeance. Therefore, actors under strong influence of Dhanishtha may do better in genres like action, comedy and tragedy; depending on their overall horoscopes.

Natives under strong influence of Capricorn part of Dhanishtha may be more interested in materialistic pursuits. On the other hand, natives under strong influence of Aquarius part of Dhanishtha may be more interested in philosophical and spiritual pursuits. It doesn't mean Aquarius type Dhanishtha natives may not earn as well as Capricorn type Dhanishtha natives. It means money and pleasures bought with it may not be the primary need for Aquarius type Dhanishtha natives, which may be the case with Capricorn type Dhanishtha natives.

Aquarius type Dhanishtha natives may be more inclined towards philosophy, music, spiritualism and understanding things on deeper levels. For example, while reading a very good book like a biography, Capricorn type Dhanishtha actor or producer may consider making a movie based on such story. In the same situation, Aquarius type Dhanishtha actor or producer may try to learn more and more from such story or biography. The thought of converting such story into a movie may not cross his mind.

It means deep down, Capricorn type Dhanishtha native may find that the best use of such book is make it into a movie, primarily for financial gains or professional success. On the other hand, Aquarius type Dhanishtha native may want to learn more and more from this book; so that he may become better as a person.

Dhanishtha natives may be good at social skills and they may know the art of making and maintaining social relationships. Accordingly, they may have big social circles. Dhanishtha natives may possess good conversational skills which may help them convince people and maintain their social circles. Dhanishtha natives may be stubborn to some extent due to strong influence of Mars on this nakshatra. Hence it may be difficult to handle them through pressure as they may refuse to comply.

They may be better handled by trying to convince them with logic or even better, by giving them time and space to decide right or wrong by themselves. When exalted Mars or Sun is placed in Capricorn part of Dhanishtha in relevant houses of horoscope; the element of adamancy may increase a lot. Such Dhanishtha natives may often be called egoistic, adamant and/or stubborn.

Here again, the best way to handle such Dhanishtha natives is by simply giving them suggestions and then leaving them alone. Over time, these natives may think over such suggestions and they may come up with good decisions in many cases. Trying to convince them again and again; or trying to pressurize them to act on some specific suggestions or instructions may be the worst ways to handle them. If someone can make Dhanishtha natives understand things in best possible manners; it is them only.

Hence give them suggestions and let them do rest of the job. Dhanishtha natives may love when they are improving themselves. However, they may resent or even retaliate when others are trying to do the same job for them. The characteristics like being adamant or egoistic may be stronger in Capricorn part of Dhanishtha and they may be milder in Aquarius part of this nakshatra.

Dhanishtha exhibits a number of characteristics. However, different natives may embrace different characteristics, depending on placements of various planets in this nakshatra, as well as depending on their overall horoscopes. Looking at planets among navagraha; Sun, Moon, Mars, Mercury and Rahu may perform better in Capricorn part of Dhanishtha. Jupiter, Venus, Saturn and Ketu may perform better in Aquarius part of this nakshatra.

Placements of malefic planets in Dhanishtha may weaken or corrupt its significances. As a result, the native may suffer from a wide variety of problems, depending on which planets are placed in this nakshatra, as well as on his overall horoscope.

Let's look at performances of various planets in various navamshas of Dhanishtha. Starting with Leo navamsha; Mars may perform very well here whereas Saturn, Venus, Mercury and Rahu may perform well but not very well here; since all of them are either weak or not strong in Leo. Sun may perform above average or well in this navamsha; since it is strong in Leo and it is very comfortable in Dhanishtha.

Moon may perform on average here whereas Ketu may perform above average in this navamsha; since Ketu is strong in Leo and it is comfortable in Dhanishtha. Jupiter may perform on average or above average here. Though Jupiter is debilitated in Capricorn; it is strong in Leo and it is very comfortable in Dhanishtha. Among navagraha; Mars may be the strongest in this navamsha. No planet may be significantly weak in this navamsha.

Looking at Virgo navamsha; Mars, Saturn, Mercury and Rahu may perform very well here whereas Venus may perform above average but not well in this navamsha. Mercury and Rahu are exalted in Virgo and Saturn is strong in Capricorn as well as Virgo. Mars is exalted in Capricorn and it is very comfortable in Dhanishtha. Venus is debilitated in Virgo and it is comfortable but not very comfortable in Dhanishtha.

Sun may perform on average or above average here and Moon may also perform on average or above average in this navamsha. Ketu may perform below average here; since it is debilitated in Virgo. Jupiter may perform poorly but not very poorly in this navamsha; since it is very comfortable in Dhanishtha. Among navagraha; Saturn and Rahu may be the strongest in this navamsha whereas Jupiter may be the weakest.

Moving on to Libra navamsha; Saturn and Venus may perform very well here whereas Mercury and Rahu may perform well or very well here. All these planets are strong in Aquarius as well as Libra. Within the sign of Aquarius, Saturn may do its best work in this navamsha. Mars may perform on average or above average in this navamsha; since it is not strong in Aquarius as well as Libra but it is very comfortable in Dhanishtha.

Moon may perform below average in this navamsha; since it is weak in Aquarius. Jupiter may perform on average here whereas Ketu may perform below average or on average in this navamsha. Sun may perform below average but not poorly in this navamsha; since it is weak in Aquarius and it is debilitated in Libra, but it is very comfortable in Dhanishtha. Among navagraha; Saturn may be the strongest in this navamsha whereas Sun may be the weakest.

Considering Scorpio navamsha; Saturn may perform well or very well here whereas Venus, Mercury and Rahu may perform well but not very well in this navamsha. Venus and Mercury are not strong in Scorpio and Rahu is debilitated in this sign. Mars may perform above average or well in this navamsha; since it is strong in Scorpio and it is very comfortable in Dhanishtha.

Sun may perform on average or above average here whereas Ketu may perform above average in this navamsha; since it is exalted in Scorpio. Jupiter may perform on average or above average here whereas Moon may perform below average in this navamsha, since it is debilitated in Scorpio and weak in Aquarius. Among navagraha; Saturn may be the strongest and Moon may be the weakest in this navamsha.

Looking at professions, natives under strong influence of Dhanishtha may be seen practicing as musicians, flute players, drum players and other professionals who play various musical instruments, actors, writers, singers, dancers, sportsmen, police officers, army officers, naval officers, air force officers, security guards and all other types of professionals dealing in security; doctors, consultants, engineers, software developers, researchers, lawyers, judges, politicians, government officers, administrators, ministers, chief ministers, prime ministers, presidents, astrologers, psychics, tantrics, professionals dealing in real estate, hotel industry, airline industry, tour and travel industry, movie industry, music industry, fashion industry, media industry, radio industry, defence industry, sports industry and many other types of professionals, depending on their overall horoscopes.

Let's look at some other facts associated with this nakshatra. Dhanishtha is considered as an active and movable nakshatra. It is considered as a female nakshatra. Vedic astrology assigns Famer Varna and ether element to Dhanishtha. The Gana assigned to Dhanishtha is Rakshasa and the Guna assigned to it is Tamasic. It is an upward nakshatra and its Yoni or animal symbol is Lion.

Shatabhisha

Shatabhisha is 24th among 27 nakshatras. All four quarters of Shatabhisha fall in Aquarius. The literal meaning of the word Shatabhisha is translated as 'hundred doctors' or 'hundred medicines'.

These meanings indicate that Shatabhisha is associated with remedies, medicines, treatments and cures. It also indicates that Shatabhisha is related to diseases and problems. This is because medicines or remedies are required only after diseases or problems have appeared. Hence Shatabhisha deals with both aspects of this field; diseases as well as remedies.

The name of this nakshatra suggests hundred medicines or doctors. It implies many things at the same time. The first one is the fact that Shatabhisha is a resourceful nakshatra, since only resourceful people may afford hundred doctors. The second one tells that the problems Shatabhisha may try to deal with may be complicated or very complicated. This is because hundred doctors or hundred medicines may be required for complicated problems only.

It means natives under strong influence of Shatabhisha may face such problems in their lives; for which they may have to try a number of remedies or options, until they find the ones which work. Hundred doctors or medicines also indicate variety. It means natives under strong influence of

Shatabhisha may face various types of problems in their lives and they may have to try various types of approaches to solve these problems. One may only need many doctors specializing in different fields, when he suffers from many problems.

Let's look at this meaning from the angle of a doctor, instead of looking at it from the angle of a patient. The name Shatabhisha suggests that natives under strong influence of this nakshatra may possess wisdom of hundred experts and they may have hundreds of resources to solve problems. The name also suggests that natives under strong influence of Shatabhisha may be skilled in hundreds of fields, which means in many fields.

Hence Shatabhisha natives may possess great expertise in their respective fields and they may at the same time possess knowledge in many other fields. Whether a native under strong influence of Shatabhisha may become a patient or doctor; depends on how the energy of this nakshatra is used in a horoscope. When Shatabhisha is occupied by suitable benefic planets in relevant houses, it may produce the best types of professionals in their fields.

It means an astrologer under strong influence of Shatabhisha may not be merely an astrologer; he may be one of the best astrologers. Such astrologer may possess great amount of knowledge and he may have hundreds of ways to solve the problems of his clients; when supported by his overall horoscope. Likewise, a doctor say a neurologist under strong influence of Shatabhisha may be known as one of the best neurologists in a region.

On the other hand, if unsuitable or malefic planets are placed in Shatabhisha in a horoscope, the native is highly likely to be a patient. It means such native under strong influence of Shatabhisha may suffer from a number of problems in certain spheres of his life; depending on placements of various planets in this nakshatra as well as on his overall horoscope.

It should be noted that great expertise is always accompanied by great confusions. This means that in order to achieve expertise in a field, you need to dig deeper and deeper. The deeper you dig, more confusing things become. If you are capable enough to get through such confusions, you may be blessed with expertise.

However, if you are lost in such confusions, you may end up even more confused than you were before you started digging. It means Shatabhisha natives may end up creating more problems for them, while trying to solve current problems. Hence Shatabhisha is a difficult to handle energy and it almost always needs to be supported by strong horoscopes in order to deliver good results.

Vedic astrology assigns an empty circle as the main symbol of Shatabhisha and this symbol renders many characteristics to this nakshatra. A circle gives the idea of containing something, within its boundaries. A circle also indicates that things inside it are separated from things outside. Most things in universe work in circles and they are not linear. A circle is not open like a line and it is a closed body. It means what is outside may not get inside easily; and what is inside may not get outside easily.

Hence characteristics like secrecy, privacy, maintaining boundaries and being introvert are exhibited by Shatabhisha. Therefore, Shatabhisha natives may not easily trust other people and they may keep maintaining certain boundaries, even after years of relationships with people. For this reason, Shatabhisha natives may prove some of the most difficult to understand natives. It means even after having years of close relationships with them, you may not claim to know them sufficiently.

There may still be many parts of their personalities which are hidden and you don't know them. For this reason, you may often not be able to assign fixed patterns to them as they may surprise you with their actions, every now and then. In deeper sense, the need for secrecy rises from insecurity. It means you try to keep those things secret, which you believe may cause problems if revealed. This belief gives birth to insecurity as you sense problems if such things are revealed. Hence you try your best not to reveal such things. It means you try to conceal them or in other words, you try to keep them secret.

Therefore, the characteristic of insecurity is also exhibited by Shatabhisha. Hence Shatabhisha natives may feel insecure about certain aspects of their lives. As a result, they may tend to keep such aspects secret. Such aspects may be different for different natives, depending on placements of various planets in Shatabhisha as well as on placement of this nakshatra in various houses of a horoscope.

For example, if a benefic combination of Sun, Mercury and retrograde Venus is placed in the tenth house of a horoscope in Aquarius and Sun is placed in Shatabhisha, the native may become an astrologer or a doctor. Both these professions deal in secrets. Apart from that, the native may be especially good at ensuring that his professional expertise is not revealed to others. It means such native may possess very good expertise in his field and he may closely guard such secrets which his competitors may be looking for.

It is like the native may have some secret formulas, the others may be trying to steal them and the native may be trying his best to save them. It should be noted that in this case, the native may be secretive related to his profession as well as related to some other aspects of his life and his entire personality may not be secretive.

However, if a combination of Sun, Mercury and Venus is placed in the first house of a horoscope in Aquarius in Shatabhisha, it is an altogether different equation. The combination is happening in the first house and the first house is the core of horoscope. As a result, the native may not be secretive in some specific spheres of his life; he may be an embodiment of secrets.

It means everything he does or says may have many layers of secrets. Such native may be considered as a walking enigma and even the people closest to him may not be able to know him sufficiently. Similarly, Shatabhisha natives may tend to keep secrets related to different spheres of their lives; depending on placements of various planets in Shatabhisha, in different houses of their horoscopes.

Looking at one more example, if a malefic combination of Venus, Rahu and Mercury is placed in the fifth house of a horoscope in Aquarius in Shatabhisha, the native may have different types of secrets. Such native may have an extramarital affair at a time and he may have a child or children from such extramarital affair. However, neither the lover nor the children of this native may be revealed to the world and they may remain hidden or secret.

Instead of having an extramarital affair, the native may also have more than one wife and family, say two wives and families; depending on his overall horoscope. However, one of the wives or both the wives may not know that the native has another wife and another family. It should be noted that such extreme results may happen only when the overall horoscope is supportive for them and not otherwise.

An empty circle also conveys the idea of a void. This void may be considered as the one which is in the background of all creation and destruction. Stars and planets are created and destroyed within time and space; however the space always remains present in the background. The beginning and end of a planet, a star or even a universe may be predicted. However when it comes to the empty space where all such creation and destruction is taking place, no one knows anything. It means no one knows when the space was created and when it will cease to exist.

The space is a void as well as the biggest secret. Everything happening in it is created and destroyed; though its own creation and destruction is unknown. Through this symbol of empty circle, Shatabhisha tries to connect to the biggest secrets of the universe. It means when occupied by suitable planets and supported by overall horoscopes; Shatabhisha may bless the natives under its influence with the ability to understand deepest secrets of universe. It means these natives may become highly evolved spiritual souls who may gain access to the deepest secrets of creation and destruction.

An alternate name of Shatataraka is also mentioned for Shatabhisha. The word Shatataraka literally translates into 'hundred stars'. This name conveys the idea that Shatabhisha may contain hundred stars within it. It means Shatabhisha natives may contain many mysteries within them. It also means that Shatabhisha natives may have qualities represented by hundred stars.

On a deeper level, it means Shatabhisha natives may possess the ability to gain complete access to deepest secrets of universe. This is because counting primarily ends at hundred and everything after that is repetition. We also measure growth or results in percentage where hundred means complete. Hence Shatabhisha natives may possess the ability to reach the deepest mysteries of the universe and beyond. As already mentioned, highly evolved spiritual natives under strong influence of Shatabhisha may gain access to the deepest secrets of nature.

Vedic astrology assigns Varuna, the god of water as the ruling deity of Shatabhisha. Influence of Varuna relates Shatabhisha to all types of water bodies, especially to the oceans. It is believed that a number of characteristics of Shatabhisha are similar to those exhibited by an ocean. An ocean is known to hide hundreds of treasures and secrets inside it. Shatabhisha also exhibits characteristics of holding hundreds of skills and secrets.

Like a circle, an ocean is also limited by its boundaries from all sides. This restricts interaction of the ocean with entities lying outside these boundaries. Looking from a deeper angle; a circle, an ocean and the void or space are complete in themselves and they don't need anything else to complete them. It means Shatabhisha exhibits the characteristic of finding such completeness from within, rather than looking for it from outside. Hence natives under strong influence of Shatabhisha may find and embrace such completeness; if their overall horoscopes are supportive. All these characteristics make Shatabhisha an introvert type of nakshatra.

Vedic astrology assigns Rahu as the planetary ruler of Shatabhisha. Rahu is known as a planet of illusions, secrets, mysteries and magical events. Influence of Rahu adds characteristics like hiding, curing, exploring and dealing with mysteries; to Shatabhisha. All four quarters of Shatabhisha fall in Aquarius, ruled by Saturn. Influences of Saturn and Aquarius add characteristics like analytical abilities, philosophical approach, patience and perseverance to Shatabhisha. The most prominent characteristic of Shatabhisha is its desire to deal with secrets and mysteries. Whether it gets lost in them or it is able to solve them; depends on the overall horoscope of the native under consideration.

Though there are other nakshatras which exhibit their love for one type of search or another, Shatabhisha is one of its own kind. For example, natives under strong influence of Ardra may have strong tendency to search and explore. However, these natives may not go to extreme limits and hence they may not get lost. At the same time, Ardra natives may also not be able to reach some of the deepest secrets.

This is because there is always the risk of getting lost, when you push yourself to extreme limits in any domain. Shatabhisha has this tendency to go all the way. In doing so, it may at times reach all the way and it may at times get lost on the way. The characteristic of aiming for the extremes or looking for the deepest secrets, makes Shatabhisha a difficult to handle energy.

When it comes to combination of planets and nakshatras, planets are able to control nakshatras more than nakshatras are able to control them, in most cases. For example, various planets may utilize the energies of nakshatras like Mrigashira, Rohini, Punarvasu, Pushya and many other nakshatras, the way they want. When it comes to Shatabhisha, the opposite may happen in many cases. Shatabhisha may control and manipulate the energy of most planets among navagraha. It means most planets may get lost on the way, instead of reaching the final destination.

Therefore, most natives under strong influence of Shatabhisha may be able to channelize its energy properly; only when there are other strong benefic planetary energies in their horoscopes. It means in most cases, planets placed in Shatabhisha may not be able to reach the deepest secrets, unless they are supported by other strong and benefic planets. In the absence of such planets, natives under strong influence of Shatabhisha may face various types of problems, depending on their overall horoscopes.

Taking an example, if a malefic combination of Mars and Rahu forms Angarak Yoga in the fourth house of a horoscope in Shatabhisha; and Sun, Jupiter and Saturn are weak or afflicted; the native may literally go insane. The native under strong influence of such Angarak Yoga formed in Shatabhisha may suffer from serious psychological disorders and he may never recover if the rest of his horoscope is not supportive.

Considering another example, if a malefic combination of Moon, retrograde Mercury, retrograde Saturn and Ketu is placed in the eighth house of a horoscope in Aquarius; and Jupiter, Sun and Mars are weak or afflicted; the native may get murdered. If two or three out of these four planets say Moon and retrograde Mercury are placed in Shatabhisha, the native may get murdered and that too anonymously. It means the murder of this native may become a mystery which may not be solved for a long period of time or forever, depending on his overall horoscope.

In an extreme case of this type when the overall horoscope is non-supportive in a specific way, even the dead body of such native may never be found. Shatabhisha deals with mysteries and the eighth house deals with mysteries as well as death. Hence a strong malefic combination in the eighth house like the aforementioned one, under strong influence of Shatabhisha can make the native die in a mysterious way.

On the other hand, if a benefic combination of Moon and Mars forms Chandra Mangal Yoga in the eighth house of a horoscope in Aquarius, with Mars in Shatabhisha; the results may change. If exalted Sun is placed in the tenth house in Aries, exalted Jupiter forms Hamsa Yoga in the first house in Cancer, exalted Saturn is placed in the fourth house in Libra; and benefic exalted Venus is placed in the ninth house in Pisces, the native may become a government officer. The native may become a successful doctor working with government or he may become an officer in an investigating agency of government; like a revenue officer or a crime investigating officer; depending on his overall horoscope.

Shatabhisha is the master of secrets. Natives under strong influence of Shatabhisha may achieve success through some hidden knowledge, faith, technique or something else which is not known to many people. Shatabhisha natives may be good at guarding secrets of other people along with their own secrets, just like an ocean guards hundreds and thousands of things, hidden deep inside it. Hence these natives may be considered trustworthy when it comes to share secrets with them.

Shatabhisha natives may know a lot many secrets of a number of people and it may not bother them. It means they may digest such secrets with ease, like the ocean. For this reason, natives under strong influence of Shatabhisha may achieve more success in professional spheres where privacy of clients is of utmost importance.

Shatabhisha natives are generally fascinated by things which are hidden and mysterious. Hence they may love solving puzzles, enigmas and mysteries. Shatabhisha natives are generally suspicious in nature and they may not trust people easily. Hence it may take them long periods of time to trust people. Shatabhisha has a natural tendency to guard and protect its boundaries like an ocean or a circle.

Accordingly, natives under strong influence of Shatabhisha may guard themselves against anything that is new and foreign. Due to this characteristic, Shatabhisha natives may take long to get intimate, even with their lovers. These natives may not share their innermost feelings with their husbands or wives; even after years of marriages. Shatabhisha natives may develop natural resistance to changes. Hence it may not be easy for them to get accustomed to new people, places or circumstances.

Due to these characteristics, Shatabhisha natives may not be considered social. It may take a lot for other people to get inside their circles of trust, due to their highly guarded boundaries. Shatabhisha natives may like to stay alone instead of being in company of other people. This characteristic may help them connect to their inner strengths, when their overall horoscopes are supportive.

However, the same characteristic may make them suffer from depression and other psychological disorders, when their overall horoscopes are not supportive. Shatabhisha natives may be good at learning new languages and hidden or mysterious sciences like astrology. Hence some of them may be seen practicing as astrologers, tantrics, psychics, spiritual gurus and healers of various types.

Shatabhisha exhibits a number of characteristics. However, different natives may embrace different characteristics, depending on placements of various planets in this nakshatra, as well as on their overall horoscopes. Looking at planets among navagraha; almost no planet on its own may be able to make the best use of energy of Shatabhisha. It means even planets like Saturn, Mercury, Venus and Rahu may feel uncomfortable in this nakshatra, though they are all very comfortable in Aquarius.

The key to perform well in Shatabhisha is held by the overall horoscope of the native under consideration. Provided the overall horoscope is supportive; Mars, Jupiter, Venus, Mercury, Saturn and Rahu may perform well in Shatabhisha. Sun and Ketu may perform well in Shatabhisha, only under specific conditions. Moon is not comfortable in this nakshatra.

To summarize, Shatabhisha is a difficult to handle energy and almost no planet may handle it on its own. Hence the secret of success for this most secretive nakshatra lies in the fact, whether or not a horoscope is supportive enough to handle it. Placements of malefic planets in Shatabhisha in a horoscope can cause various types of problems for the native, depending on his overall horoscope.

Let's look at performances of various planets in various navamshas of Shatabhisha. Starting with Sagittarius navamsha; Saturn, Rahu, Venus and Mercury may perform well but not very well here; when supported by overall horoscope. All these planets are strong in Aquarius but they are not strong or weak in Sagittarius. Mars may perform above average in this navamsha, since it is strong in Sagittarius and it has decent strength in Aquarius.

Sun may perform on average here whereas Ketu may perform above average in this navamsha. Sun is weak in Aquarius whereas Ketu has decent strength in this sign. Moon may perform below average here, since it is weak in Aquarius, not strong in Sagittarius and uncomfortable in Shatabhisha. Jupiter may perform above average in this navamsha, since it is strong in Sagittarius and it has decent strength in Aquarius. Among navagraha; Saturn may be the strongest in this navamsha whereas Moon may be the weakest.

Looking at Capricorn navamsha; Saturn, Venus, Mercury and Rahu may perform well or very well here; when supported by overall horoscope; since all of them are strong in Aquarius as well as Capricorn. Mars may perform above average here and if supported by overall horoscope; it may perform well in this navamsha.

Sun may perform on average here whereas Moon may perform on average or below average in this navamsha. Moon is weak in Aquarius and it is uncomfortable in Shatabhisha. Ketu may perform on average in this navamsha whereas Jupiter may perform below average here, since it is debilitated in Capricorn. Among navagraha; Saturn may be the strongest and Jupiter may be the weakest in this navamsha.

Moving on to Aquarius navamsha; Saturn, Venus, Rahu and Mercury may perform well or very well here; when supported by overall horoscope. Mars may perform on average here whereas Sun may perform below average in this navamsha; since Sun is weak in Aquarius. Jupiter may perform on average in this navamsha and if supported by overall horoscope, it may do better than that.

Ketu may perform on average in this navamsha and it may perform below average when it is not supported by overall horoscope. Moon may perform poorly here. Within the sign of Aquarius, Moon may deliver its worst performance in this navamsha. Though it is debilitated in Scorpio navamsha of Dhanishtha, it is comfortable in Dhanishtha whereas it is uncomfortable in Shatabhisha. Hence it may do better in Scorpio navamsha of Dhanishtha; within the sign of Aquarius. Among navagraha; Saturn may be the strongest in this navamsha whereas Moon may be the weakest.

Considering Pisces navamsha; Venus and Saturn may do well or very well here whereas Mercury and Rahu may perform above average but not well in this navamsha. Venus is exalted in Pisces whereas Mercury as well as Rahu is debilitated in this sign. Mars may perform on average in this navamsha and if not supported by overall horoscope, it may perform below average here.

Sun may perform below average here whereas Ketu may perform above average in this navamsha. Sun is not strong in Pisces whereas Ketu is exalted in this sign. Moon may perform on average and if supported by overall horoscope; it may perform above average in this navamsha. Jupiter may perform above average in this navamsha; since it is strong in Pisces. Among navagraha; Saturn and Venus may be the strongest in this navamsha whereas Sun may be the weakest.

Looking at professions, natives under strong influence of Shatabhisha may be seen practicing as consultants, advisors, psychics, astrologers, paranormal mediums, healers, magicians, black magicians, tantrics, spiritual gurus, astronomers, space researchers, scientists, analysts, astronauts, pilots, air force officers, ocean explorers, naval officers, treasure hunters, scuba divers, coast guards, doctors, physicians, surgeons, neurologists, psychiatrists, chemists, ayurvedic doctors, homeopathic doctors, engineers, software developers, architects, interior designers, politicians, lawyers, judges, writers, journalists, bloggers, professionals dealing in airline industry, shipping industry, chemical industry, pharmaceutical industry, medical industry, media industry, movie industry, television industry; and many other types of professionals, depending on their overall horoscopes.

Let's look at some other facts associated with this nakshatra. Shatabhisha is considered as an active and movable nakshatra. It is considered as neutral in gender. Vedic astrology assigns Shudra Varna and ether element to Shatabhisha. The Gana assigned to Shatabhisha is Rakshasa and the Guna assigned to it is Tamasic. It is an upward nakshatra and its Yoni or animal symbol is a female horse.

Poorvabhadrapada

Poorvabhadrapada is 25th among 27 nakshatras. The first three quarters of Poorvabhadrapada fall in Aquarius whereas the last quarter falls in Pisces.

The word Poorvabhadrapada literally translates into 'the former lucky feet' or 'the former one with lucky feet'. In general, the meaning of this word is considered to add characteristics like being fortunate and lucky, to Poorvabhadrapada.

Looking deeper, the journey of nakshatras from Ashwini to Revati is the journey of soul from its first birth to liberation. Hence Ashwini represents the basic instincts necessary for survival. On the other hand, the previous nakshatra Shatabhisha represents strong urge to know the deepest secrets of existence. Hence great deal of evolution is witnessed from Ashwini to Shatabhisha.

Poorvabhadrapada is the beginning of the final chapter of this journey. Poorvabhadrapada is the first nakshatra where the urge to live everything in order to know the real thing reaches its peak. Shatabhisha wants to know but it may not want to live everything. It means when a native under strong influence of Shatabhisha learns a substance is toxic or poisonous, he may not wish to go further.

Hence this information in itself may be sufficient for him and he may not wish to taste such substance, in order to actually know it. Though we may claim information as knowledge, these two words are much different from each other, in spiritual terminology. Something that you learn through other sources but you have no personal experience with it is called information. Something that you have personally experienced may only be called knowledge in the deepest sense.

It means when a Shatabhisha native knows poison is harmful and he wishes to stay away from it, this is information and not knowledge, in spiritual terminology. Poorvabhadrapada is the first nakshatra which is not happy with information and it wants knowledge. Accordingly, Poorvabhadrapada becomes an even more difficult to handle nakshatra than Shatabhisha. The information that poison is harmful may not be sufficient for a Poorvabhadrapada native and he may wish to experience it. This urge to live and know through experience makes Poorvabhadrapada a highly volatile nakshatra and literally anything is possible with this nakshatra.

For this reason, Poorvabhadrapada is one of the most feared nakshatras. Natives under strong influence of Poorvabhadrapada may be seen living at polar extremes, depending on the working of this nakshatra in their horoscopes. The head of a big terrorist organization and a high authority law enforcement officer dedicated to destroy such organization; may both be under strong influence of Poorvabhadrapada.

A native completely lost in materialistic extremes like alcohol, drugs and sex; and a highly evolved spiritual native who may be just a step away from liberation; may both be under strong influence of Poorvabhadrapada. The working of this nakshatra is so confusing and extreme that it is labelled as the most difficult to handle nakshatra by many Vedic astrologers. As we discover its symbol and ruling deity, the reasons for such fears may become obvious.

Since the journey of liberation is closer to its end, nothing less than extremes should be expected. Even a simple video game or a sports competition becomes very difficult or extreme towards the end. The same happens here also. The first 24 nakshatras have enjoyed, gained information, lived some of such information and left what they thought might be problematic. Poorvabhadrapada is the sum total of all these nakshatras and it often wishes to live each and everything; rather than gaining information about it.

An ascetic under strong influence of Poorvabhadrapada may engage in extreme practices like standing on one foot for many years, not eating for many days, sitting or lying on thorns and other such extreme practices. He is not doing it for fun; he is simply an extremist. It means he may go to any lengths to achieve what he believes in. Hence if someone tells him that by standing on one foot for two years, he may achieve his goal; he may do so without giving it second thought. Due to this characteristic of living at the extremes, Poorvabhadrapada natives may often become active members of one type of extremist group or another.

Though all this may look troublesome and it may not seem to bear any resemblance to the meaning of the word Poorvabhadrapada, it does make perfect sense. Poorvabhadrapada is the first step on the first path, where gaining information becomes insufficient and knowledge alone will do. The dark side of this path is that one may have to go through extremely bad or evil experiences on this path. The bright side is that from such experiences alone, true knowledge and wisdom is born.

It is nothing but fair that no one may know sin better than a sinner. The one who hasn't sin may never know in reality, the kind of fire every sin initiates within. Such fire continuously burns the sinner from inside and through this suffering only; the purest desire for redemption as well as that for staying away from sin is born. Though one may think the ultimate destination may be reached without engaging in sins at all, it may not be so in reality.

Until you have sinned and then experienced the hell it brings with it; you may never get rid of it. Someone who has never engaged in a sin may simply have no idea why it is bad and how bad it may be. Hence he may always be lured by sins, since it is human nature to taste the prohibited fruit. Liberation means freedom from every desire and urge. Until you have sinned, suffered and moved on; the desire to try forbidden things may always be there.

With this desire, you may never be able to achieve liberation. It seems surprising that the thing which is stopping you from achieving liberation is the fact that you have the desire to sin but you don't. Actions don't count at all on this path; and only intentions or desires do. As long as this curiosity or desire is there, there is no scope of liberation. Poorvabhadrapada wishes to live each and every sin it wants to commit, suffer punishment, understand how it actually works and then leave it for good.

Once you have tried something, disliked it completely and left it; there is no chance you are going back to it. Until you have tried it; there is always a chance or desire to try it. Technically, the last part of leaving sins and desires for good doesn't happen in Poorvabhadrapada and it happens in the next nakshatra Uttarabhadrapada. Hence Poorvabhadrapada is the attempt to try everything. This attempt tells it what is to be kept and what is to be left. The keeping and leaving part then happens in Uttarabhadrapada.

Hence Poorvabhadrapada is the first step on the final path. First step here means the first part. This path has two parts where the first part deals with knowing everything through personal experiences. The second part brings the final wisdom, guiding what to keep and what to leave. Since the final path is undoubtedly the luckiest path; the meaning 'first lucky feet' should better be understood as 'first part of the luckiest path'.

The main symbol assigned to Poorvabhadrapada is 'the front two legs of a funeral cot'. Fearsome it may seem, this symbol also indicates first part of the journey beyond death. It means Poorvabhadrapada is willing to take this first step and it is willing to cross this first part; which takes it beyond death; to liberation. Achieving victory over death requires dealing with it first. Hence Poorvabhadrapada exhibits characteristics like being dangerous, violent, volatile, versatile, dramatic, daredevil, adventurous, extremist and secretive. All these characteristics help Poorvabhadrapada complete the challenges it may face during the first part of the final path.

Another important as well as relevant symbol is associated with Poorvabhadrapada. This symbol represents a 'two faced man'. One of his faces belongs to a gentle, civilized and well cultured person whereas the second face represents a violent, destructive, evil and mysterious person. This symbol indicates that Poorvabhadrapada has the ability to live at opposite extremes at the same time. It means natives under strong influence of Poorvabhadrapada may lead dual lives. One part of these lives is the public face whereas the other one is the hidden face.

Hence an average marketing executive who in reality is a government secret agent or spy; may very well be a Poorvabhadrapada native. A tourist guide, who turns out to be the mastermind of a bomb blast incident; may also be a Poorvabhadrapada native. A religious guru who engages in sex, drugs and alcohol during the dark hours of night; is very likely to be a Poorvabhadrapada native. A well reputed doctor dealing in trafficking of human organs; may be a Poorvabhadrapada native. Similarly, all other such natives who are leading dual lives may be under strong influence of Poorvabhadrapada.

This is because Poorvabhadrapada represents an extreme battle between the God and the Devil. In other words, Poorvabhadrapada represents an extreme battle between conscience and ego. The journey of liberation is in its final stage in Poorvabhadrapada. Hence it is natural for the Devil to use his best weapons, in order to win this battle. The God and the Devil are the good and the evil inside a Poorvabhadrapada native; and they are engaged in the decisive battle.

This is why Poorvabhadrapada features two opposite extremes at the same time. There are no doubts that the goodness will prevail in the end. However, the next stage represented by Uttarabhadrapada may or may not be achieved in present lifetime, by a Poorvabhadrapada native. If the overall horoscope is supportive, natives under strong influence of Poorvabhadrapada may finally win this battle. Such Poorvabhadrapada natives may get rid of all evil and they may be left with goodness alone. This stage announces the arrival of second step or second part of the final path. It means such Poorvabhadrapada native may get promoted to an Uttarabhadrapada type native.

The horoscope of Saint Ramakrishna Paramahamsa is a good example of benefic use of energy of Poorvabhadrapada.

Exalted Venus forms Malavya Yoga in the first house of this horoscope in Pisces in Uttarabhadrapada; and Revati rises in the ascendant. A combination of Moon, retrograde Mercury and Sun is placed in the twelfth house in Aquarius, with Moon in Poorvabhadrapada and Sun as well as retrograde Mercury in Shatabhisha.

Retrograde Jupiter is placed in the fourth house in Gemini in Ardra. Rahu is placed in the third house in Taurus, Ketu is placed in the ninth house in Scorpio, retrograde exalted Saturn is placed in the eighth house in Libra and exalted Mars is placed in the eleventh house in Capricorn. The horoscope features strong influence of Ardra, Shatabhisha, Poorvabhadrapada, Uttarabhadrapada and Revati. All these nakshatras except Revati deal with search and realization of higher self. Due to a strong combination of planets in extreme nakshatras like Shatabhisha and Poorvabhadrapada; his search for the final truth was absolutely extreme. Apart from that; the twelfth house is the most extreme house of horoscope.

Placement of exalted Venus in the first house in Uttarabhadrapada explains his unmatched love and devotion for goddess Kali. Placement of Venus in Uttarabhadrapada explains he was finally blessed by the goddess to reach Uttarabhadrapada stage. Later on, the saint was also able to reach the final stage which is represented by Revati; rising in the ascendant. The life of this highly respected and loved saint was full of extreme acts. He behaved like a child at one moment and he became wise the next moment.

He tried a number of different methods to reach the final destination, just to check if all of them worked. He embraced the feminine side of nature so extremely that he actually grew breasts. An incident says that one day he put a sword to his head and he said to goddess Kali that he would behead himself, if the goddess didn't show up and blessed him. It is said the goddess blessed him on that day. His life was full of such extremes; due to strong influence of Poorvabhadrapada.

On the other hand, some Poorvabhadrapada natives may not win this battle during their present lives, due to their overall horoscopes. Such Poorvabhadrapada natives may be seen living at extremes throughout their lives; without reaching the next stage. If that happens, the journey is continued in their next lives also; until they get through this stage during one of their future lives.

Vedic astrology assigns Aja Ekapada as the ruling deity of Poorvabhadrapada. The word Aja Ekapada literally translates into 'a goat with one foot'. This god is believed to be a Rudra form of Lord Shiva. Hence Aja Ekapada connects Poorvabhadrapada to Rudra form of Lord Shiva; the form which is known for destruction.

Goats have been used for sacrifices since ancient times. Head is taken as a representative of ego since ego is believed to reside in head. Hence this god may imply that in order to cross the first part of the final path, one must get beheaded. It means one must completely get rid of ego in order to get through the first part of the final path. When a decisive battle with ego begins; it is natural for things to express themselves on extreme levels.

Ego is the first as well as the last entity which stops one from achieving liberation. It means ego possesses us and distracts us so that we may walk on any path but the final path. Despite its best efforts; if it fails to stop us from treading on that path; it may attack us with everything it has.

It should be noted that with liberation, ego alone is destroyed and nothing else is. Soul is untouchable and the body dissolves itself into the five elements; only to form again. Hence the journey to liberation is the journey to get rid of ego. When this journey reaches the first part of the final path; it becomes a matter of life and death for ego. The conscience is trying to get rid of ego in order to cross this part whereas the ego is trying its best to survive by creating various types of illusions, in order to confuse the native. Since this is the final battle, things touch extremes and the atmosphere becomes volatile. As a result, Poorvabhadrapada natives may often oscillate between polar extremes.

Vedic astrology assigns Jupiter as the ruling planet of Poorvabhadrapada. The association of the most benefic planet among navagraha with a seemingly evil nakshatra like Poorvabhadrapada confuses some astrologers. In the deepest sense, Jupiter alone is capable of ruling Poorvabhadrapada. Among other things, Jupiter signifies conscience; and spiritual growth achieved through conscience.

When the decisive battle is fought between conscience and ego; more and more conscience is required to defeat ego. It is perhaps due to Jupiter's influence only; that Poorvabhadrapada may finally win this battle and cross this part of the final path. Hence a native under strong influence of Poorvabhadrapada may keep engaging in extremes; realizing their wastefulness in the end. If Jupiter is benefic as well as strong and the overall horoscope is supportive, the native may finally win this battle and cross this part of the final path.

The first three quarters of Poorvabhadrapada fall in Aquarius ruled by Saturn whereas the last quarter of Poorvabhadrapada falls in Pisces ruled by Jupiter. These planets and signs add characteristics like indulgence, awareness, conscience, intelligence, patience, repentance, penance and realization to Poorvabhadrapada. The realization comes after indulgence, awareness and repentance.

The indulgence, awareness and repentance may happen in Aquarius part of Poorvabhadrapada whereas realization may come in Pisces part of Poorvabhadrapada. Awareness in this context means the native may be aware of whatever good or bad he may be engaging in. After engaging in the evil, awareness may create the need for repentance and penance. The native may purify himself through these processes and then the realization may come.

It is the realization that each time you engage in bad karmas, regrets and guilt are built. To get rid of them, you have to go through repentance and penance. Hence the realization tells you it is better not to engage in bad karmas in the first place, instead of going through this process again and again. This means it is better to retain purity than to corrupt it and regain it through troublesome processes. This is when you may get rid of ego since ego is in the root of all bad karmas.

To be precise, ego is in the root of all good and bad karmas as long as you are the doer. It should be noted that this realization can only be earned and it can't be learned. The one who has actually been burnt by fire may truly realize the agony it inflicts. The one who has only seen other people getting burnt may never realize the true potential of such agony; though he may think he does. Therefore, realization is meaningful only if it comes as a result of your own experiences and not otherwise.

Poorvabhadrapada natives may be good at balancing opposite sides of their personalities. These natives are masters of disguise. For this reason, criminals under strong influence of Poorvabhadrapada may prove to be the most difficult types of criminals to handle. Shravana type criminals may also be difficult but they are not difficult to handle; and they are difficult to trace or catch. Shravana natives may keep working under the radar and they may not engage in acts of violence. Even when they are caught, they may use legal and diplomatic methods to get out. When it comes to Poorvabhadrapada natives; the first challenge is to trace their true identities.

Poorvabhadrapada natives may not be hidden in literal sense and in most cases; they may be hiding in plain sights. It means a Poorvabhadrapada type criminal may be right before your eyes the entire time but you may not be able to recognize him; let alone catch him. Even if you catch a Poorvabhadrapada type criminal, he may prove extremely difficult to handle. Poorvabhadrapada natives may not be scared of death and this puts them in positions of advantage. It means one such criminal may attack you and kill you instead of getting caught.

Even if he is killed during the process; he may not care. Even if you capture him alive, he may keep creating problems for you, every now and then. For instance, he may get your family kidnapped or harmed and ask for his release. Criminals under strong influence of Poorvabhadrapada are generally blessed with large networks of people. Hence they may trouble you a lot; even if they are behind bars or restricted through other means.

Poorvabhadrapada natives may be so skilled at disguising themselves that it may be hard; even for cleverest people to detect the true shades of their personalities. For example, a Poorvabhadrapada type college professor who has very good reputation and who is considered as a thorough gentleman preaching others to be good; may actually be a spy, a secret agent or a militant; depending on his overall horoscope. Hence natives under strong influence of Poorvabhadrapada are likely to have hidden sides of personalities and such hidden sides may be opposite to the visible sides of their personalities. In most cases, the hidden sides may be their true sides and the visible sides may be cover-ups.

The symbol of a sword or a double-edged sword is also assigned to Poorvabhadrapada. This symbol also represents characteristics like destructive potential and dual-nature. Hence duality becomes the most prominent characteristic of Poorvabhadrapada. Poorvabhadrapada natives may fool people by pretending to be fools themselves.

Taking an example, if a native carrying something illegal in his vehicle stops at a police post and asks a policeman the way to somewhere, pretending as if he is lost; he may be a Poorvabhadrapada native. In general, the police may randomly stop and check vehicles. Hence people often try to avoid them by pretending they are not able to see them. The police also know that most people try to avoid them and hence they may take interest in stopping some of these people.

The last thing many policemen may expect is someone looking for them and asking them something. In most cases, such an act causes distraction as the policeman is busy thinking about how to guide this native properly. At the same time, he may subconsciously assume that this native is genuine since he is not afraid of police and he seems to be lost. A Poorvabhadrapada native may ask for directions and he may leave, thanking the policeman for his helping spirit. This is what you should expect when you're dealing with a native under strong influence of Poorvabhadrapada.

These natives may be intelligent, adventurous and brave. However, they may hide this side of their personalities and they may pretend to be average type of natives or even less than average. The best way to find them is by spotting their ability to observe. Poorvabhadrapada natives may be continuously observing their surroundings, hiding this act from other people.

For example, a Poorvabhadrapada type clerk may seem engaged in his day to day file work, with his head down. However when observed carefully, you may find that his entire body is much more alert than it should be while doing such work. If you try to get closer, the tension in his body as well as his level of alertness may increase. Once you enter the zone which is too close for him; he may suddenly stand up; as if he wishes to go to wash room or somewhere else. This Poorvabhadrapada native may be apprehending an attack and hence he is getting out of a vulnerable position. You have better chances of attacking him while he is seated. Hence he may stand up and become ready for an apprehended attack.

This happens because natives under strong influence of Poorvabhadrapada may lead dual lives. Doing so creates insecurity that someone may know about them and catch them. It is the fear of getting caught which means the instinct of survival which makes them so alert and observant all the time. Due to their ability to balance opposite extremes and have dual personalities, natives under strong influence of Poorvabhadrapada may become very successful as actors, if supported by their overall horoscopes.

Actors under strong influence of Poorvabhadrapada may be especially known for playing wide variety of characters and you may simply not be able to fit them into a specific type. Hence an actor who plays a terrorist, a cop, a doctor, a wrestler, a common man, a comedian, a serious character and various other characters with the same ease; may be under strong influence of Poorvabhadrapada.

Poorvabhadrapada natives are generally good at socializing though they may do so only in order to be parts of the crowd. Poorvabhadrapada natives may be skilled at the art of keeping low profiles; to avoid getting special attention.

When you get special attention, people may get interested in you and they may wish to know more and more about you. Since Poorvabhadrapada natives may not want you to know more and more about them; they may avoid getting special attention.

Hence instead of finding them in front rows or in the last rows; you may find them seating in the middle rows; becoming parts of the crowd. Front rows draw maximum attention and there is an element of suspicion associated with last rows. However, no one bothers much about middle rows and this is where Poorvabhadrapada natives may be found. The rows in this context relate to various spheres of life. It means Poorvabhadrapada natives may be found in the middle in most cases; looking like common men. This is because they know that playing common man is the safest option. We generally take interest in very good people and/or very bad people. However, almost no one may take interest in a common man.

Poorvabhadrapada exhibits a wide variety of characteristics. However, different natives may embrace different characteristics, depending on placements of various planets in this nakshatra, as well as on their overall horoscopes. Looking at planets among navagraha; Sun, Saturn, Mercury, Mars, and Rahu may perform better in Aquarius part of this nakshatra. Jupiter, Venus, Moon and Ketu may perform better in Pisces part of this nakshatra. Among navagraha; Sun may not be comfortable in this nakshatra.

It should however be noted that Jupiter and Saturn become the most important planets for natives under strong influence of Poorvabhadrapada. If both these planets are weak, malefic, afflicted or corrupted in a horoscope; the native under strong influence of Poorvabhadrapada may not be able to cross the first part of the final path during his present life.

However, if both Jupiter and Saturn are strong and benefic; the native has good chances of crossing the first part of the final path; provided the rest of his horoscope is supportive. Sun and Mars may also help Poorvabhadrapada natives reach their targets; though they may not be as important as Jupiter and Saturn in most horoscopes.

It should be noted that different natives may feel the impact of characteristics of Poorvabhadrapada in different domains; depending on the placement of this nakshatra in various houses of their horoscopes; as well as on their overall horoscopes. For example, if benefic Mercury is placed in the tenth house of a horoscope in Aquarius in Poorvabhadrapada; its characteristics may primarily affect the professional sphere of the native.

Hence the entire personality of this native may not be influenced by Poorvabhadrapada. As a result, the native may have hidden ways of making money through profession, he may engage in illegal professions along with legal professions, he may become an actor, or he may have more than one profession at the same time; depending on his overall horoscope.

Considering another probability, if a combination of Venus and retrograde Saturn is placed in the seventh house of a horoscope in Aquarius in Poorvabhadrapada; the equation may change. The first wife of this native may have a personality type, which may be opposite to that of the native. This may cause serious problems in marriage and the marriage may dissolve in the end.

The second wife of the native may also have a personality type, significantly different from that of the native as well as from that of his first wife. If the second marriage fails due to his overall horoscope and the native gets married again;

the same may happen. It means the native may always end up marrying women with opposite personality types. Hence all his marriages may require him to strike balances between his personality and those of his wives.

However, if a combination of retrograde Mercury and Rahu is placed in the first house of a horoscope in Aquarius in Poorvabhadrapada; it is a different equation. Most characteristics of Poorvabhadrapada may prominently reflect through the entire personality of the native. As already mentioned, the first house of horoscope is its core and energies registered in this house may reflect throughout the personality of the native. Since planets like Mercury and Rahu are placed in Poorvabhadrapada, the native may become a spy, a secret service agent, a private detective, a drug dealer or a terrorist; depending on the rest of his horoscope.

In the same horoscope, if benefic exalted Saturn is placed in the ninth house in Libra along with benefic Jupiter; benefic Sun is placed in the twelfth house in Capricorn along with Moon in Dhanishtha, benefic retrograde exalted Venus is placed in the second house in Pisces in Uttarabhadrapada; and Mars is placed in the fifth house in Gemini in Ardra, the native may become a spiritual guru. The native may achieve very good spiritual growth and if the finer factors in his horoscope are supportive, he may be able to cross the first part of the final path; represented by Poorvabhadrapada.

Placements of malefic planets in Poorvabhadrapada may cause various types of problems for the native, depending on his overall horoscope. When Poorvabhadrapada is occupied by malefic or corrupted planets in a horoscope in relevant houses; the native may suffer from various types of psychological problems. Since natives under strong influence of Poorvabhadrapada may have more than one side of personality; not all of these natives may be able to balance them properly. The most common outcome may be psychological disorders.

When the overall horoscope is troubled, natives under strong influence of Poorvabhadrapada may especially be vulnerable to psychological disorders like schizophrenia. This disorder makes the sufferer have two sides of personality. One of them is his regular side and the other one possesses him at times; without his knowledge or control. This is why it is called split personality disorder also.

In this case also, Poorvabhadrapada is playing its role well; blessing the native with two sides of personality. The only difference is that the native is not able to switch these sides at his own will and the sides switch themselves without his will or control; creating panic and problems. Poorvabhadrapada natives with supportive horoscopes are able to control these sides and they make such transitions only when they want.

Let's look at performances of various planets in various navamshas of Poorvabhadrapada. Starting with Aries navamsha; Saturn, Venus, Mercury and Rahu may perform well but not very well in this navamsha. Saturn is debilitated in Aries whereas Venus, Mercury and Rahu are not strong in Aries. Mars may perform above average or well in this navamsha, depending on overall horoscope.

Sun may perform on average but not well in this navamsha; since it is weak in Aquarius and it is not comfortable in Poorvabhadrapada. Jupiter may perform above average or well here whereas Ketu may perform above average in this navamsha. Both Ketu and Jupiter are strong in Aries but Jupiter is more comfortable in Poorvabhadrapada than Ketu. Moon may perform on average in this navamsha. Among navagraha; Rahu may be the strongest in this navamsha. No planet may be significantly weak in this navamsha.

Looking at Taurus navamsha; Saturn, Venus, Mercury and Rahu may perform well or very well in this navamsha. All these planets are strong in Aquarius as well as Taurus. Within the sign of Aquarius; Rahu may deliver its best performance in this navamsha. It is strong in Aquarius, it is exalted in Taurus and it has great comfort in Poorvabhadrapada.

Mars may perform on average or above average in this navamsha whereas Sun may perform on average or below average here. Jupiter may perform on average or above average here whereas Moon may perform above average in this navamsha. Ketu may perform below average in this navamsha; since it is debilitated in Taurus. Among navagraha; Rahu may be the strongest in this navamsha whereas Ketu may be the weakest.

Moving on to Gemini navamsha; Saturn, Venus, Mercury and Rahu may perform well or very well in this navamsha. All these planets are strong in Aquarius as well as Gemini. Sun may perform below average here whereas Mars may perform on average in this navamsha. Moon may perform on average or below average here whereas Jupiter may perform on average in this navamsha.

Ketu may perform below average or poorly here; since it is not strong in Aquarius, it is weak in Gemini and it is not much comfortable in Poorvabhadrapada. Among navagraha; Saturn and Rahu may be the strongest in this navamsha whereas Ketu may be the weakest.

Considering Pisces navamsha; Jupiter may perform very well here whereas Venus, Ketu and Moon may perform well or very well in this navamsha. Jupiter is strong in Pisces and it is exalted in Cancer. Within the sign of Pisces, Jupiter as well as Moon may be the strongest in this navamsha. Venus and Ketu are exalted in Pisces and they have decent strength in Cancer.

Sun may perform on average or below average here whereas Mars may perform below average in this navamsha. Sun is weak in Cancer and Mars is debilitated in this sign. Apart from that; none of them is strong in Pisces. Saturn may perform on average in this navamsha since it is not strong in Pisces as well as Cancer. Mercury may perform poorly here whereas Rahu may perform below average in this navamsha. Though both of them are debilitated in Pisces; Rahu is somewhat stronger in Cancer than Mercury; and it is more comfortable in Poorvabhadrapada than Mercury. Among navagraha; Jupiter may be the strongest in this navamsha whereas Mercury may be the weakest.

Looking at professions, natives under strong influence of Poorvabhadrapada may be seen practicing as spies, detectives, secret agents, police officers, army officers, naval officers, air force officers, administrative officers, revenue officers, diplomats, coffin makers, cemetery keepers, arms manufacturers, arms dealers, scientists, doctors, engineers, IT professionals, software developers, astrologers, black magicians, psychics, tantrics, aghoris, healers, spiritual gurus, religious gurus, actors, TV artists, stage artists, dancers, writers, singers, musicians, directors, producers, sportsmen, criminals, murderers, serial killers, contract killers, researchers, explorers, politicians, professionals dealing in weapon industry, defence services, terrorist organizations, mafia, media industry, movie industry, television industry, music industry, airline industry, hotel industry, fashion industry, casino industry, tobacco industry, liquor industry, chemical industry, medical industry, pharmaceutical industry and many other types of professionals; depending on their overall horoscopes.

Let's look at some other facts associated with this nakshatra. Poorvabhadrapada is considered as a passive and fierce nakshatra. It is considered as a male nakshatra. Vedic astrology assigns Brahman Varna and ether element to Poorvabhadrapada. The Gana assigned to Poorvabhadrapada is Manava and the Guna assigned to it is Sattwic. It is a downward nakshatra and its Yoni or animal symbol is Lion.

Uttarabhadrapada

Uttarabhadrapada is 26th among 27 nakshatras. All four quarters of Uttarabhadrapada fall in Pisces. The literal translation for the word Uttarabhadrapada is 'the latter lucky feet'. Accordingly, it is believed that Uttarabhadrapada blesses the native with luck and fortune.

As already discussed in previous chapter named Poorvabhadrapada, the term feet here represents steps and the steps represent a journey. It was seen that a more relevant meaning of the word Poorvabhadrapada may be 'the first part of the lucky path'. This lucky path is the final path of liberation and it has two parts. The first part is covered in Poorvabhadrapada which practically experiences a number of good and evil things. After indulgence, it creates the need for repentance and penance which help it reach realization. Hence this realization is the fruit or essence, which is received after awarely going through indulgence, repentance and penance. This fruit called realization helps Poorvabhadrapada reach the second part of the final path; called Uttarabhadrapada.

In the journey of a soul for liberation, Poorvabhadrapada and Uttarabhadrapada represent two parts of the final stage or the final path. Poorvabhadrapada receives the fruit of realization. This realization teaches it that it is better not to engage in bad karmas in the first place. Once engaged, the purity of the soul is corrupted and it needs to be retained through processes of repentance and penance, conducted with awareness. The last quarter of Poorvabhadrapada falling in Pisces achieves this realization and the next part of the final path, called Uttarabhadrapada begins.

In Uttarabhadrapada, the realization is turned into wisdom. Hence wisdom is the primary characteristic exhibited by Uttarabhadrapada. This wisdom is achieved through personal experiences and that is why it is of supreme value. In the deepest sense, wisdom can only be achieved through personal experiences and not otherwise. Just like Poorvabhadrapada is the sum total of all previous nakshatras; Uttarabhadrapada is also the same. It is the sum total of all previous nakshatras, including Poorvabhadrapada.

Hence Uttarabhadrapada represents that stage in the journey of a soul, which has been achieved after awarely going through everything. The realization gained through such experiences blesses it with wisdom. As a result, there is no other nakshatra like Uttarabhadrapada, when it comes to discriminate between the good and the evil, necessary and unnecessary; and between all other polar extremes. The beauty of Uttarabhadrapada is that it does so effortlessly; means naturally. For this reason, Uttarabhadrapada is called the wisest among all nakshatras. Hence natives under strong influence of Uttarabhadrapada may be some of the wisest people.

The challenge posed by the first part of the final path is to achieve realization after personal experiences. Once this task is completed in Poorvabhadrapada, the next and the last part of the final path begins. The task for this part is to use wisdom for the wellbeing of the universe. Hence Uttarabhadrapada has the task of spreading wisdom instead of enjoying it alone. It is like a student has completed the final course of his studies and he is now left with one job only; to teach others.

Since spreading wisdom is the final task before the journey comes to an end; natives under strong influence of Uttarabhadrapada may form a high percentage of those spiritually enlightened souls who are supposed to enlighten others. It means many of the spiritually most enlightening teachings may be delivered by natives under strong influence of Uttarabhadrapada.

One of the most revered saints Shri Ramakrishna Paramahamsa was born with exalted Venus placed in the first house of his horoscope in Pisces in Uttarabhadrapada; and Revati rises in the ascendant. He received final wisdom through goddess Kali as represented by exalted Venus in Uttarabhadrapada in the first house. He then enlightened the world with his spiritual teachings.

Shree Osho Rajneesh is known for delivering some of the spiritually most enlightening discourses in the recent years. His horoscope features Rahu in the fourth house in Pisces in Uttarabhadrapada, and five planets in ascendant in Sagittarius. Retrograde exalted Jupiter is placed in the eighth house in Cancer. It is important to note that most of these discourses were delivered during the planetary period of Rahu which was in effect for 18 years from 1969 to 1987. This period was followed by Jupiter's planetary period which was in effect till his death.

Shri Guru Nanak is another highly enlightened spiritual soul who blessed us with a highly enlightening spiritual discourse, Shri Japji Saheb. His horoscope features exalted Venus in Pisces in Uttarabhadrapada and exalted Jupiter in Cancer in Pushya.

One of the prevalent horoscopes of Lord Krishna features the placement of Jupiter in the eleventh house in Pisces. Though the nakshatra of placement of Jupiter is not mentioned; it is highly likely to be Uttarabhadrapada. This is because no other planet may be as capable of delivering one of the spiritually most enlightening discourses; as Jupiter in Uttarabhadrapada.

Hence the primary task for Uttarabhadrapada is to spread wisdom or enlightenment; depending on the overall horoscope under consideration. Though Revati represents the peak of all nakshatras, it is generally not interested in actions. Enlightened souls under strong influence of Revati may support universal balance, in more passive and subtler ways. On the other hand, natives under strong influence of Uttarabhadrapada may actively engage in acts of restoring balance; depending on their overall horoscopes.

Uttarabhadrapada represents the final part of the final path. Hence the primary job here is not to learn, but to teach. Applying this fact to various fields of life; natives under strong influence of Uttarabhadrapada may be seen practicing as spiritual gurus, religious gurus, astrologers, consultants, advisors, counsellors and all other professionals who guide people.

Wisdom, the main characteristic of Uttarabhadrapada, is different than cleverness, intellect and intelligence. Cleverness is the characteristic of Mercury, where one looks at the small picture, primarily in order to gain some type of advantage. Intellect is also represented by Mercury and it is the ability to understand something through logic or reason. Intellect also helps with usage of such information later on, as and when required.

It means intellect may help us gain and store information though it may not help acquiring knowledge through real experiences; especially in domains like spiritualism. Hence spiritual teachers under strong influence of Mercury may not have themselves witnessed divine experiences. They are more likely to learn what highly enlightened souls have delivered and then they may teach what they have learnt. Their teachings may not be their own experiences; and they are likely to teach what is mentioned in books or in other types of discourses. A number of scholars and religious teachers may fall in this category. This is because they may be merely repeating what was experienced by someone else; without applying such experiences to their own lives.

The characteristic of intelligence is represented by Sun and Jupiter. It is the ability to learn new things and make decisions without having previous experiences. It means a native under strong influence of Mercury may deal with all such situations which he is familiar with. However, he may find it difficult to deal with situations which are new and which may be entirely different from what he has learnt. On the other hand, a native under strong influence of Sun or Jupiter may be fully capable of handling such situations.

Sun and Jupiter don't depend much on storing information and they believe more in spontaneity, guided by intelligence. A typical Mercury type student may be comfortable as long as an examination is set from within the syllabus. However, he may not be able to do much if there are some questions which are out of syllabus. Sun and Jupiter may be able to handle such questions without much trouble.

It means Mercury believes in preparing itself properly for future events. On the other hand, Sun and Jupiter believe in being prepared all the time. This means they generally don't depend on specific preparations as they understand that new situations may often show up. Hence intelligence is more like the ability to learn and handle things; as and when they appear.

When it comes to wisdom, it is above all these characteristics. Wisdom in its purest form is collectively represented by Jupiter and Saturn; among navagraha. Wisdom is directly proportional to conscience which is the characteristic ruled by Jupiter alone. Jupiter helps you grow conscience and then conscience helps you achieve spiritual growth. The result of spiritual growth is delivered in the form of wisdom. It is the ability which guides you how to use intellect, intelligence, cleverness, expertise and all likewise qualities.

You may be intellectual, clever and/or intelligent but you may use these characteristics for selfish motives, if you don't have wisdom. Intellect and intelligence are more like tools or weapons and they don't know how to be used. In the wrong hands, they may often end up causing destruction. Wisdom guides you when to use these characteristics and how to use them. Wisdom will always work for universal wellbeing, even when it is engaging in acts of war. Lord Krishna says the war (Mahabharata war) is absolutely necessary for peace; a perfect example of wisdom.

Saturn deals with characteristics like perseverance, patience and experience. These characteristics help the conscience in achieving wisdom. Hence wisdom may be considered as the sum total of best characteristics of Jupiter and Saturn. Jupiter guides what to do and Saturn ensures execution. Jupiter guides what to avoid and Saturn ensures compliance. Together, these two planets form a perfect pair; like the one formed by Lord Krishna and Arjuna. Lord Krishna guides and Arjuna complies. This is why Jupiter and Saturn are considered as the two most important planets for spiritual growth.

Hence it should come as no surprise that Saturn is the planetary ruler of Uttarabhadrapada and all four quarters of this nakshatra fall in Pisces, ruled by Jupiter. As a result, Uttarabhadrapada is under strong influence of Saturn and Jupiter. Jupiter and Saturn bless Uttarabhadrapada with characteristics like wisdom, patience, perseverance, contentedness, the ability to stay unaffected by circumstances, speech abilities, kindness, generosity, love for the entire existence; and a number of other characteristics.

Vedic astrology takes the main symbol of Uttarabhadrapada as the back part of a funeral cot. As already seen in Poorvabhadrapada, the symbol is the front part of a funeral cot. The funeral cot represents the journey beyond death, the journey of liberation. The front part of the cot indicates the first part of the final path for liberation. The second part represented by Uttarabhadrapada indicates the stage when liberation has been achieved. However, the native is supposed to act as a teacher now, before finally retiring; where the retirement happens in Revati.

Hence Uttarabhadrapada represents the stage where the soul is liberated but it is engaging in the task of spreading enlightenment. Therefore, Uttarabhadrapada is not a student but it is a teacher who wishes to educate a number of students before his retirement. This is why majority of highly enlightening spiritual discourses have been delivered by natives under strong influence of Uttarabhadrapada. These souls are kind. They have achieved liberation and before the final retirement, they wish to thank the entire existence for supporting them in their journeys. Hence they express such gratitude by restoring balance and by giving people gems of wisdom.

Vedic astrology assigns Ahir Budhanya as the ruling deity of Uttarabhadrapada. According to Vedic mythology, Ahir Budhanya is considered as a serpent god who lives far beneath the earth. Some Vedic scholars believe that Ahir Budhanya lives deep down under the sea. Ahir Budhanya is considered wise and far more compassionate deity in comparison to Aja Ekapada, the ruling deity of Poorvabhadrapada.

Vedic astrology assigns Lord Shiva as the final presiding deity of Uttarabhadrapada. Lord Shiva is considered to deal with affairs beyond death, including liberation. It is interesting to see that Lord Shiva connects to Poorvabhadrapada as well as to Uttarabhadrapada through their ruling deities. However, Aja Ekapada is considered as a Rudra form of Lord Shiva whereas Ahir Budhanya is considered as a benevolent form of Lord Shiva.

Relating it to the discussion in Dhanishtha; Aja Ekapada represents Rudra Tandava whereas Ahir Budhanya represents Ananda Tandava. The ego has been destroyed in Poorvabhadrapada through Rudra Tandava and it is now the time to engage in Ananda Tandava. Uttarabhadrapada represents this Ananda Tandava.

Uttarabhadrapada natives may be capable of looking at the bigger picture. Hence they may not work for selfish motives and they may instead work for the benefits of the others. In most cases, Uttarabhadrapada natives may also end up benefitting from such acts. For example, if two parties approach an Uttarabhadrapada native for mediation, he may come up with a solution which is fair to both parties. The parties may accept such solution and they may also give him something in return, though he may not have been doing anything for personal gains.

Uttarabhadrapada natives may often receive gifts, which is due to the gratitude people wish to show to them. Such gratitude is there because such Uttarabhadrapada natives may guide and help them every now and then, without expecting anything in return. In case of highly evolved souls under strong influence of Uttarabhadrapada, such gifts may come through divine sources, though they may come through worldly sources also.

Uttarabhadrapada natives are generally content type of natives and they may not desire for more and more. Despite these characteristics, they may often have much more than they need. Uttarabhadrapada is very good at blessing the natives under its strong influence with great fortunes which may belong to this world and/or they may belong to higher worlds, depending on their overall horoscopes. Uttarabhadrapada is a very versatile nakshatra and it is capable of behaving in any manner it finds fit according to a situation. It means Uttarabhadrapada is as skilled at the art of disguise as Poorvabhadrapada, though the former may almost always do so for higher motives.

For this reason, natives under strong influence of Uttarabhadrapada may be the most difficult to predict natives, among all 27 nakshatra type natives. This is because wisdom has been achieved. Hence these natives may not live life with fixed rules and they may make new rules every day or every moment, according to what situations demand. In the deepest sense, they may not make any rules at all, as they may understand that life is much bigger than any rule. Hence whatever life throws at them, they may read the situation and act accordingly.

Lord Krishna promises he won't use any weapon during the war and then one day, he summons the all powerful weapon Sudarshana to kill Bheeshma. The beauty of this incident is that he is as comfortable in breaking the promise, as he was in making it. Lord Krishna's life is full of such incidents which make him defy rules and promises every now and then. In reality, he only acted according to the need of situations and nothing else. In the deepest sense, keeping your word is an act of ego, especially when it may cost fortunes to your loved ones. Lord Krishna was far too wise to be fooled by ego. Hence he made and broke promises with the same ease.

Let's take an incident from Lord Buddha's life. On a specific day, three different natives approached him at different times and they asked the same question; 'does God exist'? Lord Buddha said no to the first native, he said yes to the second one and he kept quiet in the third case. His disciple Ananda raised curiosity that though the question was same, why did he give three different answers?

Lord Buddha said the question looked the same but it was not. The first person came with strong belief that God existed. However, he had no personal experience and he simply wanted Lord Buddha's approval so that he may stop searching. Hence Lord Buddha said no to shatter his belief so that he might actually engage in search of God instead of satisfying himself with plain words.

The second native came with a strong belief that God did not exist and Lord Buddha shattered his belief also, so that he might engage in search instead of stopping this noble quest with some words. The third native was actually in search of God and he wanted motivation from Lord Buddha. Hence Lord Buddha said nothing to him, conveying everything through silence.

He conveyed to this native that a true searcher should not find comfort in words and he should engage in efforts. Hence he conveyed that God was not something to be learnt through others, it was something to be personally experienced. Though the first two natives left confused, the third native understood and he left after paying gratitude to Lord Buddha.

This is how difficult Uttarabhadrapada natives may be to fit into a box. Even the cleverest person may not be able to make sense of such acts of Lord Krishna and Lord Buddha, though they make perfect sense. Hence Uttarabhadrapada natives may be highly unpredictable and they may behave in any manner, according to the need of situation. There are no rules in the domain of Uttarabhadrapada and it simply operates through conscience and wisdom.

Uttarabhadrapada natives may be fixed towards their goals and they may try their best to achieve such goals. However, they may not be in hurry, they may not get obsessed with goals and they may not engage in selfish acts to accomplish such goals. Uttarabhadrapada natives may not be bothered if they are not able to achieve their goals, despite their best efforts. They may simply move on to other goals, as if it is all a game. For them, sincere and genuine efforts may be all that counts and results may not. In deeper sense, it means Uttarabhadrapada is focused on karma and it doesn't bother about results. This is one of the most valuable lessons taught by Lord Krishna through Bhagwat Gita. This lesson says, engage in best possible karmas and don't wish for fruits.

In the deepest sense, these native may be able to get all the fruits from the acts of engaging in karmas themselves. When you are playing for fun and you are enjoying a lot, what do you get when the game ends? You don't get anything in the end and you get everything during the act of playing itself. Hence the wisdom represented by Uttarabhadrapada teaches that karma itself should be your fruit. It means you should be completely absorbed in your karmas.

This way, you may enjoy each and every moment while engaging in karmas; and the desire for fruits may not be formed at all. This is why Uttarabhadrapada natives may find it easy to move on to next goals, if they fail to achieve some of them. They may try their best, they may enjoy every moment of their efforts and they may not care much about results. Karmas may indeed be fruits for them.

Uttarabhadrapada natives generally radiate strong vibes of safety and friendliness. Hence most people may feel safe in their companies even when they may be meeting them for first or second times. Uttarabhadrapada natives may be good at seeing things as they are; which means without prejudice. Hence they may prove very good as advisors, guides or gurus of various types.

For this reason, people in their social circle may often contact them for advices, primarily for two reasons. The first one is the fact that they may be wise enough to give such advices. Secondly, these natives may be completely selfless while giving such advices. For instance, suppose a friend approaches an Uttarabhadrapada native with a profitable business proposal and asks him whether such native or a common friend should become a part of this venture.

If such Uttarabhadrapada native feels that the common friend is more suitable for this job, he may say so. Though it may cost him a profitable opportunity, he may not even care to realize. This is because all he may care for is that if someone has approached him for advice, he should impartially deliver him the best possible advice. Hence such Uttarabhadrapada native may only care for doing his best while delivering advice. Once again, he is enjoying the karma itself and he doesn't care for results. It means the act of giving advice may itself be a sufficient reward for him.

Due to these characteristics, Uttarabhadrapada natives may be well respected by their families as well as by people in their social circles. Since Uttarabhadrapada natives may often put wellbeing of others before them, they may seem to suffer losses at times; though they may not think so. However, other people may realize this with time and they may start honoring them with gifts and gratitude from time to time.

A true saint doesn't want any materialistic benefits and he only wishes to work for universal wellbeing. However, all types of people are willing to shower them with gifts and gratitude. This is because such people realize that such saint is unselfishly working for their benefits. Hence they feel strong urges to give him something in return. When they say goodness brings goodness, it almost always comes true in Uttarabhadrapada.

Uttarabhadrapada natives are inclined towards social causes. Hence they may be found working for various charitable organizations or making big donations to such organizations. Uttarabhadrapada natives may have keen interest in fields related to supernatural and paranormal. Some of these natives may practice in such fields.

Uttarabhadrapada natives are more likely to engage in soft fields like astrology, numerology, palmistry, spiritualism, yoga, meditation and some soft forms of tantra. However, they may not wish to engage in fields like black magic, fierce forms of tantra, aghorism and other practices which are generally considered dark. These fields may demand sacrifice of various animals at times and Uttarabhadrapada natives may not be comfortable with this concept.

Uttarabhadrapada natives are generally content in nature and they may try to live happily, even under adverse circumstances. Uttarabhadrapada natives generally have forgiving natures. Such natives may believe in giving more chances to wrong doers so that they may improve. Uttarabhadrapada natives may not be opposed to evil people;

they may be opposed to their evil deeds. Their wisdom may guide them not to hate anyone.

Hence an Uttarabhadrapada native may strongly oppose many of your actions and he may even stand against them; but he may still love you. Such native is not against you, he is against your actions. Uttarabhadrapada natives may be wise enough to understand that the actions of a person and the complete existence of that person are different. Hence they may not hold your actions against you.

Due to their forgiving natures, Judges under strong influence of Uttarabhadrapada may announce punishments or penalties which may be somewhat less than what convicts deserve, depending on the gravity of the offences committed by them. However, they may almost never announce punishments which are even slightly more than what convicts may deserve, depending on the cases.

Likewise, a native under strong influence of Uttarabhadrapada may not believe in improving his son by punishing him or by imposing conditions on him. He may instead advise him and then give him time to improve by himself. Uttarabhadrapada natives may be peace loving and violence may be their last resort. However, such peace may come from inner strength and not from cowardice or weakness.

Therefore, when violence is the only option left, they may engage in it whole heartedly. They may put such display of violence or aggression that most people may be shocked; as they may not have expected such acts from these natives; given their peaceful and forgiving nature. This makes Uttarabhadrapada natives very difficult to understand and predict. You simply can't put them in any personality type since they may be carrying all possible personality types within them.

Lord Krishna goes to Kaurvas as a peace messenger before the final war and he asks for five villages only, instead of asking for the entire empire of Pandvas, as per the promise made by Kaurvas. He asserts that peace is of utmost value and he will convince Pandvas to stay away from war, even if five small villages are given to them. The request is denied and the war begins. While engaging in war, Lord Krishna motivates Arjuna to kill anyone and everyone who comes between him and victory. He says this victory and hence this violence is necessary for peace.

If any nakshatra can complete both these extreme and opposite tasks with same ease, it is Uttarabhadrapada. Though a nakshatra like Uttarashada may complete the second task with ease, it may not feel at ease with the first task; that of requesting for five villages in order to avoid war. What makes the first task even more difficult is that Lord Krishna is fully capable of winning this war in no time; yet he is requesting to grant five villages to avoid war. This is an act that no other nakshatra may perform as well as Uttarabhadrapada. By virtue of these characteristics, Uttarabhadrapada natives may be respected and loved by people around them. They may seldom wish to command but people may wish to be commanded by them.

Uttarabhadrapada exhibits a number of characteristics. However, different natives may embrace different characteristics, depending on placements of various planets in this nakshatra, as well as depending on their overall horoscopes. Looking at planets among navagraha; Sun, Moon, Jupiter, Venus, Mars, Saturn and Rahu are comfortable in Uttarabhadrapada. Mercury and Ketu are not comfortable in this nakshatra.

Placements of malefic planets in Uttarabhadrapada may weaken or corrupt its characteristics. As a result, the native may suffer from a number of problems; depending on his overall horoscope. For example, a malefic combination of Mars, retrograde Saturn and Rahu placed in the tenth house of a horoscope in Pisces in Uttarabhadrapada may corrupt its significances. As a result, the native may pretend to be a very good person though he may be selfish.

Depending on the rest of his horoscope, the native may become a fake religious guru, a fake spiritual guru, a fake astrologer or a criminal. The native may be good at forming charitable trusts and raising funds for welfare of weaker sections. However, he may use most of the donations and gifts received by such trusts for selfish motives.

Let's look at performances of various planets in various navamshas of Uttarabhadrapada. Staring with Leo navamsha; Jupiter, Venus and Ketu may perform well or very well here, depending on overall horoscope. Sun and Mars may perform above average here whereas Moon may perform well in this navamsha. Moon is strong in Pisces, it has decent strength in Leo and it has great comfort in Uttarabhadrapada.

Saturn may perform on average but not below average in this navamsha. Saturn has decent strength in Pisces, it is weak in Leo and it has great comfort in Uttarabhadrapada. Mercury may perform below average or poorly in this navamsha and Rahu may also do the same. Mercury is stronger than Rahu in Leo whereas Rahu is more comfortable in Uttarabhadrapada than Mercury. Among navagraha; Jupiter may be the strongest in this navamsha whereas Mercury and Rahu may be the weakest.

Looking at Virgo navamsha; Jupiter may perform well or very well here whereas Venus and Ketu may perform well but not very well in this navamsha; since both of them are debilitated in Virgo. Moon may perform well here since it is strong in Pisces and it has decent strength in Virgo. Sun may perform on average or below average here whereas Mars may perform on average in this navamsha.

Saturn may perform above average in this navamsha, since it is strong in Virgo. Mercury may perform on average or below average here whereas Rahu may perform on average in this navamsha. Within the sign of Pisces; Rahu and Mercury may be the least weak in this navamsha. Among navagraha; Jupiter may be the strongest in this navamsha whereas Mercury may be the weakest.

Moving on to Libra navamsha; Jupiter and Venus may perform very well here whereas Ketu and Moon may perform well but not very well in this navamsha. Mars may perform on average or above average here whereas Sun may perform below average in this navamsha, since it is debilitated in Libra.

Saturn may perform above average or well here; since it is exalted in Libra and it has great comfort in Uttarabhadrapada. Mercury may perform below average here whereas Rahu may perform on average in this navamsha. Among navagraha; Venus may be the strongest in this navamsha whereas Mercury may be the weakest.

Considering Scorpio navamsha; Jupiter and Ketu may perform very well here whereas Venus may perform well or very well in this navamsha. Ketu is exalted in Pisces as well as Scorpio. Mars may perform well in this navamsha whereas Sun may perform above average here.

Saturn may perform on average or above average here whereas Moon may perform on average in this navamsha, since it is debilitated in Scorpio. Mercury as well as Rahu may perform poorly in this navamsha. Rahu is debilitated in Pisces as well as Scorpio. Among navagraha; Jupiter and Ketu may be the strongest in this navamsha whereas Mercury and Rahu may be the weakest.

Natives under strong influence of Uttarabhadrapada may be seen practicing as yoga instructors, astrologers, numerologists, palmists, vastu experts, saints, spiritual healers, spiritual gurus, religious gurus, religious teachers, preachers, counselors, advisors, teachers, financial consultants, natives working with charitable organizations, judges, administrators, politicians, religious leaders, reformers, bankers, doctors, scientists, engineers, researchers, explorers, discoverers, astronomers, astronauts, actors, musicians, singers, dancers, writers, poets, sportsmen; professionals dealing in hotel industry, airline industry, travel industry, movie industry, television industry, radio industry, music industry, medical industry, pharmaceutical industry, information and technology field, software industry, telecom industry, internet industry, event management industry, match making services, matrimonial services; and many other types of professions; depending on their overall horoscopes.

Let's look at some other facts associated with this nakshatra. Uttarabhadrapada is considered as a balanced and fixed nakshatra. It is considered as a male nakshatra. Vedic astrology assigns Kshatriya Varna and ether element to Uttarabhadrapada. The Gana assigned to Uttarabhadrapada is Manava and the Guna assigned to it is Tamasic. It is an upward nakshatra and its Yoni or animal symbol is Cow.

Revati

Revati is the last among 27 nakshatras. All four quarters of Revati fall in Pisces. The literal translation for the word Revati is 'wealthy'. Accordingly Vedic astrology associates Revati with characteristics like accumulation of wealth, happening of good events and leading good life.

Vedic astrology considers a fish or two fish swimming in water as the main symbol of Revati. Revati marks the completion of journey of liberation. Poorvabhadrapada represents the first part of the final path and Uttarabhadrapada represents the last part of the final path. Hence Poorvabhadrapada deals with extreme learning and Uttarabhadrapada deals with highest forms of teaching. After learning the highest wisdom and after teaching it, the teacher or guru is now supposed to retire. The retirement happens in Revati.

Revati is the sum total of all nakshatras. Hence it possesses characteristics of all nakshatras. However, unlike Uttarabhadrapada, Revati may not exhibit all of these characteristics. Having something and showing it are two differing aspects. Revati is good with the first aspect and it may simply not be interested in the second aspect. A teacher needs all his skills polished as long as he is teaching. After retirement, it is of no use to polish them. The teacher may rather tend to forget them, so that he may enjoy his peace which comes with retirement.

Among all 27 nakshatras, Revati is simply incomparable to any nakshatra with the exception of Uttarabhadrapada. It means no other nakshatra except Uttarabhadrapada may even be considered for comparison with Revati as it is simply out of their league. Let's try to understand the difference between the working of Uttarabhadrapada and Revati.

The soul has already been liberated in Uttarabhadrapada and hence there is nothing more left to achieve. When you have achieved everything relevant that can be achieved and there is nothing left to achieve, you only have two options left. The first option is to hold on to what you have achieved whereas the second option is to start losing what you have achieved. Uttarabhadrapada represents the first option and Revati represents the second option.

Hence Revati doesn't tend to achieve more than Uttarabhadrapada since there is nothing more to achieve; it tends to lose. The loss here is not the loss of abilities and characteristics but it is the loss of will to use them. Revati possesses all the characteristics possessed by Uttarabhadrapada but it generally has a tendency, not to use most of them. Hence Revati may seem to possess less than Uttarabhadrapada, it is not so in reality.

The difference between Uttarabhadrapada and Revati is very subtle but obvious. Though both these nakshatras represent liberated souls, their working is different. Uttarabhadrapada is willing to actively work for the benefit of the others whereas Revati does so passively. Uttarabhadrapada may try to restore balance by actively engaging in actions when required. On the other hand, Revati is passive and it may simply not be interested in restoring any type of balance through actions.

Due to these characteristics, Revati may seem to possess less than Uttarabhadrapada. However, its strength lies in possessing less and to be precise; in exhibiting less. Revati doesn't bother about actively restoring the balance as it knows the balance will ultimately be restored, even without its active help. Hence it keeps watching everything like a viewer instead of being a participant. In deeper sense, Revati does participate in restoring balance, but not actively.

Let's add another angle to understand this difference in a better manner. The state of liberation makes you achieve your optimum potential. To be precise, the state of liberation is reached when you achieve your optimum potential. However, this state doesn't change your basic nature. When it comes to basic nature, souls are divided into two broad categories.

The first category represents the souls who are active according to their basic nature. The second category represents the souls who are passive according to their basic nature. Though both types of souls may ultimately reach liberation, their expressions are different; because of the difference in their basic natures. The state of liberation offered by Uttarabhadrapada is for the natives having active nature. On the other hand, the state of liberation offered by Revati is for the natives having passive nature. Though both these types are liberated, their expressions and even their ways of reaching may be different.

Uttarabhadrapada believes in engaging in Nishkaam karmas, which means karmas without the desires for results. By doing so, it is not bound by the fruits whether good or bad; and hence it is liberated. When it comes to Revati, it has a tendency of not engaging in karmas in the first place. Hence Revati too is not bound by fruits. This topic is as deep as any topic can get and hence, we will leave it here for the time being, in order to move on with the main topic.

Due to this difference in basic natures; most Avatars and highly enlightened souls known for blessing mankind with highest forms of wisdom and also known for making active efforts to restore balance; are likely to be under strong influence of Uttarabhadrapada. Liberated souls under strong influence of Revati may often go unnoticed. This is because activity is required to get you noticed. When you are not interested in that much activity even; you may simply go unnoticed.

Hence the classical image of a saint staying at his ashram and praying for universal wellbeing belongs to Revati. Saints under strong influence of Revati may create all the healing and goodness through their prayers; which too may be passive. It means they may not arrange big setups and they may simply make prayers by themselves. Revati believes that the energy itself is sufficient to bring about changes and nothing else may be required.

However, a saint under strong influence of Uttarabhadrapada is a warrior saint due to his active basic nature. Hence he is trying to restore balance, more through his actions, than through his prayers. Both types of souls complement each other perfectly, though it may not be visible. While Uttarabhadrapada type souls are engaging in actions to restore balance, Revati type souls are sending them more and more energy through their auras. Hence they work in perfect harmony.

A solar panel converts the energy of Sun into electrical energy. We use this energy to benefit in many ways. This solar panel is useful as well as appreciated and we pay for it. However, this fact may go unnoticed that it gets its strength from the sun through its rays. The sun acts passively in this case and hence it often goes uncredited. However, you simply can't imagine a solar panel working without an external source of energy like Sun.

This may now give you the idea that it is the Sun which is actually doing all the work. However, you simply can't use Sun's energy as electrical energy, without the help of a solar panel. It means a solar panel and Sun work in combination and they may both lose their relevance without each other, when it comes to produce electrical energy. In this combination, Sun is passive or taken for granted whereas solar panel is active and hence it seems to do all the work. Uttarabhadrapada is like the solar panel and Revati is like the Sun. Hence both these nakshatras may seem different; they work in perfect combination, complementing each other completely.

Lord Rama received a number of divine weapons from various saints who never used them. He also received an invisible Kavach (armor) before the final battle with Ravana. These saints gave such weapons and Kavach to Lord Rama as they knew he would need them during the final war with Ravana. Lord Rama used those weapons and the Kavach to put an end to the kingdom of evil.

Has this fact ever been realized that all those saints were equally important for achieving the final victory over evil. Lord Rama represents Uttarabhadrapada and hence he engaged in actions to restore balance. All such saints represent Revati. They had such weapons for long periods of time but they had no intentions of using them. When Lord Rama appeared, all of them handed their weapons over to him, so that he might win the final war.

It means Revati transferred its energy to Uttarabhadrapada so that the latter may succeed in restoring balance. The saints were passive but they were still participating in the act of restoring balance. The combination of Uttarabhadrapada and

Revati works in most mysterious ways. Both these nakshatras always form a team, to restore balance.

Looking into the symbol of two fish, these fish are moving opposite to each other. Some depictions show they are moving in a circle with each one having its head near other's tail. The opposite moving fish indicate two opposite sides of most aspects of life. It means they represent the good and the evil, happiness and sadness, day and night, life and death; and all other such phenomena. Revati is the nakshatra which embraces these seemingly opposite extremes at the same time.

Hence Revati exhibits the same level of comfort whether it faces the good or the evil, day or night, prosperity or poverty and all other such phenomena. It may now be easy to understand that, why true saints welcome bad people as well as good people. They are guided by Revati and Revati simply doesn't discriminate. Such lack of discrimination doesn't rise from lack of the ability to discriminate since they are completely capable of discriminating. This lack rises from their unwillingness to discriminate.

Hence they can discriminate but they won't. This is why saints may embrace bad people in the same way as they accept good people. In the domain of Revati, good may change into bad and bad may change into good. This is what the symbol of fish moving in a circle represents. Day keeps changing into night and night keeps changing into day. Hence they don't judge people for their evil deeds since they know every evil will ultimately turn into good. Since they know this final truth that bad keeps changing into good and good keeps changing into bad; they embrace them both.

Vedic astrology assigns Pushan as the ruling deity of Revati. Pushan is considered as a solar deity in Vedic mythology. He is supposed to bring light wherever it is needed. Pushan is also known as a god who gives wealth and prosperity. All these characteristics of Pushan are relayed through Revati. These characteristics make natives under strong influence of Revati capable of showing light of wisdom, enlightenment and happiness to others.

Vedic astrology assigns Mercury as the ruling planet of Revati. The influence of Mercury adds Mercurial characteristics like communication skills, analytical nature, trade skills and sense of humor to Revati. All quarters of Revati fall in Pisces ruled by Jupiter. Hence Revati comes under the influence of Pisces and Jupiter. These influences add characteristics like benevolence, kindness, hope, faith, wisdom, contentedness, intelligence, creativity and many other characteristics to Revati. It should be noted that the influence of Jupiter and Pisces on Revati is much stronger than that of Mercury. Jupiter is very strong in Pisces and Mercury is debilitated in Pisces.

It may seem strange why the planet of intellect represents the last nakshatra and that too under the supervision of Pisces and Jupiter, since they both promote faith, conscience and wisdom over intellect. In the deepest sense, the journey of liberation is the journey of growing faith. Intellect stands in opposition to emotions, psychic perception, faith and divine intervention. This is because intellect is comfortable only when it can assign reasons and it can reach the source.

This is why modern science is primarily based on intellect. It believes what can be explained and it may deny what can't be. However, the domains of emotions, psychic perception, faith and divine guidance come without explanations. All of them may tell you certain things from within; commonly known as intuitions of various types. Whether you embrace them or reject them, they won't supply you with reasons.

Looking at Mercury, Ashlesha is the first nakshatra ruled by it and this nakshatra falls in Cancer, the sign of emotions. Jyeshtha is the second nakshatra ruled by Mercury and it falls in Scorpio, the sign of psychic perception. Revati is the third and final nakshatra ruled by Mercury and it falls in Pisces, the sign of faith and divine guidance. It indicates that Mercury or intellect is given the task to deal with and embrace emotions, psychic perception, faith and divine guidance.

This means that in a deeper sense, the journey of liberation is primarily meant for intellect. This is because emotions, psychic perception, faith and divine guidance work well with each other. However, intellect is generally opposed to all of them. The journey of liberation is the journey to become one from inside. It means one is supposed to remove all conditions and partitions inside. Since the biggest partition is created by intellect, it is the journey of intellect. It means intellect needs to learn to accept emotions, psychic perception, faith and divine guidance, in order for this journey to be completed.

When it comes to feed ego, nothing feeds it better than intellect. Emotions may at times stand against it since an emotion like love may compel one for complete surrender; and complete surrender means death of ego. Psychic perception, faith and divine guidance come and grow on their own and they can't be controlled by ego. Hence ego conducts most of its operations through intellect. It means in a deeper sense, the journey to destroy ego is the journey to save intellect from serving for ego and unite with the other entities.

When we look at it from this angle, it comes as no surprise that Mercury reaches its state of debilitation in Pisces, the sign of liberation. It should be noted that Mercury is the only planet among navagraha which gets debilitated in a sign, which features its nakshatra. It means no other planet gets debilitated in a sign which features its nakshatra. Even the other signs which feature nakshatras ruled by Mercury are not comfortable for Mercury.

All these facts indicate that the journey of liberation is indeed the journey of intellect. It means when ego is finally destroyed in Poorvabhadrapada, the intellect surrenders and it starts working in harmony with emotions, psychic perception, faith and divine guidance. Since intellect is debilitated now, it is of no use to ego.

This brings us to one more realization. The journey of liberation can't be completed with the help of intellect and one needs emotions and faith. As long as you are trying to complete this journey with the help of intellect, you may only end up making your ego stronger. Stronger is the intellect, stronger is the ego. This is why the final act of liberation is unconditional surrender which goes against intellect as well as ego. Intellect can't surrender to something or someone, until their superiority is literally proved. When it comes to ego, it simply hates surrender. Unconditional surrender and acceptance of divine governance is liberation.

Since Revati possesses so many characteristics, natives under its strong influence may achieve success in a wide variety of fields, related to materialistic as well other domains, like spiritualism. The primary characteristics which define Revati are acceptance and contentedness. Hence natives under strong influence of Revati may be happy with what they have and they may be good at accepting whatever comes their way.

The naming of last three nakshatras has been done in mysterious ways and the names don't actually mean what they literally mean. We have already seen this in case of Poorvabhadrapada and Uttarabhadrapada. Revati literally means 'wealthy'. However, this wealth should not be confused with materialistic wealth. The last three nakshatras purely deal with spiritual terminology. Hence the meaning of Revati in this context is 'one who has achieved the ultimate wealth'. The ultimate wealth is the one which can't be taken away, once it is accumulated. This means it is the wealth of wisdom, acceptance, love, contentedness and finally; the wealth of peace.

All these characteristics are exhibited by Revati. Hence natives under its strong influence have general tendency to be loving, wise, content, forgiving and peaceful. Possession of ultimate wealth doesn't mean Revati can't possess material wealth. It simply means Revati may not be that much interested in such wealth. However, Revati is a very blessed and resourceful nakshatra. Hence natives under its strong influence may accumulate as much materialistic wealth as any other nakshatra type natives may.

The next characteristic which is strongly exhibited by Revati is passivity. Hence Revati natives may not be known for being active. Most of these natives may love rest and peace. Therefore, Revati natives are likely to do well in fields which don't need much physical exertion and aggression. At the same time, Revati natives may be gifted with creative and learning abilities. As a result, many natives under strong influence of Revati may be seen practicing in creative fields or fields like astrology, spiritualism, teaching, coaching and consultancy.

Revati natives are generally very optimistic and they continue to move towards their goals despite failures and setbacks. Revati natives may have very good imagination. Characteristics like optimism and imagination may bless them with very good results when their overall horoscopes are supportive. However, when planets like Sun, Jupiter, Mars and Saturn are weak or afflicted, Revati natives may be limited to dreams only. It means such Revati natives may be very good at making plans, but they may not engage in necessary efforts to execute such plans.

For this reason, Revati natives are also known as dreamers. When their horoscopes are supportive, all their dreams may come true. However when their horoscopes are not supportive, all they may have are dreams. Revati natives may have the tendency to build their own worlds of dreams and imaginations. In some cases, such natives may completely get lost in their worlds of dreams and they may not engage in actions to realize such dreams.

Revati natives are generally cultured and civilized. They know how to live and behave in civilized societies. These natives may possess good communication skills. Revati natives may be good at helping their friends and relatives. They may also be fortunate enough to receive help and support from their friends and relatives, whenever they may be in need.

Compassion and good fortune may be other characteristics possessed by natives under strong influence of Revati. Many Revati natives may believe that doing good to others will bring good to them and this may hold true for many of them. Revati natives may be good at understanding emotions of other people. Hence they may help them during troublesome times by sharing their pain. Many natives under strong influence of Revati may be associated with charitable organizations to help weaker sections of society.

Revati possesses a number of characteristics. However, different natives may embrace different characteristics, depending on placements of various planets in this nakshatra, as well as on their overall horoscopes. Looking at planets among navagraha; Jupiter, Venus, Moon, Mars, Saturn and Ketu are comfortable in Revati, though their levels of comfort are different. Sun, Mercury and Rahu are not comfortable in Revati. Placements of malefic planets in Revati may cause a number of problems for the native; depending on his overall horoscope.

Let's look at performances of various planets in various navamshas of Revati. Starting with Sagittarius navamsha; Jupiter, Venus and Ketu may perform very well here whereas Moon may perform well in this navamsha. Moon is strong in Pisces, it has decent strength in Sagittarius and it is very comfortable in Revati. Sun may perform on average here whereas Mars may perform above average or well in this navamsha. Both Sun and Mars are not strong in Pisces and they are strong in Sagittarius. However, Sun is not comfortable in Revati whereas Mars is comfortable but not very comfortable in this nakshatra.

Saturn may perform on average here whereas Mercury and Rahu may perform poorly or very poorly in this navamsha. Though Mercury rules Revati; it is not comfortable in this nakshatra. Likewise, Rahu is also not comfortable in this nakshatra. Apart from that, both of them are debilitated in Pisces and they are not strong in Sagittarius. Among navagraha; Jupiter may be the strongest in this navamsha whereas Rahu may be the weakest.

Looking at Capricorn navamsha; Venus may perform very well here, Ketu may perform well or very well here; and Jupiter may perform well but not very well in this navamsha, since it is debilitated in Capricorn. Moon may perform well in this navamsha and Mars may also perform well here. Mars has decent strength in Pisces and it is exalted in Capricorn. Sun may perform on average or below average in this navamsha.

Saturn may perform above average but not well in this navamsha; since it is not strong in Pisces, it is strong in Capricorn and it is comfortable but not very comfortable in Revati. Mercury as well as Rahu may perform on average or below average in this navamsha. Among navagraha; Venus may be the strongest in this navamsha whereas Mercury and Rahu may be the weakest.

Moving on to Aquarius navamsha; Jupiter, Venus and Ketu may perform well or very well here. Jupiter and Ketu have decent strength in Aquarius whereas Venus is strong in this sign. Jupiter, Venus and Ketu are all very comfortable in Revati. Moon may perform above average but not well in this navamsha, since it is weak in Aquarius. Mars may perform on average here whereas Sun may perform below average in this navamsha. Sun is not strong in Pisces, it is weak in Aquarius and it is not comfortable in Revati.

Saturn may perform above average in this navamsha, since it is strong in Aquarius. Rahu may perform on average here whereas Mercury may perform on average or below average in this navamsha. Rahu is stronger than Mercury in Aquarius. Among navagraha, Venus may be the strongest in this navamsha whereas Mercury may be the weakest.

Considering Pisces navamsha; Jupiter, Venus and Ketu may perform very well here. Venus as well as Ketu is exalted in Pisces and they are very comfortable in Revati. Jupiter is strong in Pisces and it is very comfortable in Revati. Moon may be strong here but it may not perform well in this navamsha; since it forms Gandmool Dosh here. Hence Moon may be strong but troubled in this navamsha.

Mars may perform on average here whereas Sun may perform on average or below average in this navamsha. Saturn may perform on average in this navamsha whereas Mercury and Rahu may perform very poorly in this navamsha. Among all 108 navamshas of 27 nakshatras; Mercury and Rahu may be the weakest in this navamsha. Rahu faces double debilitation in case of its placement of Scorpio navamsha of Anuradha also; within the sign of Scorpio. However, Rahu is very comfortable in Anuradha whereas it is not comfortable in Revati. Hence it may be the weakest here. Among navagraha; Venus may be the strongest in this navamsha whereas Rahu and Mercury may be the weakest.

Looking at professions, natives under strong influence of Revati may be seen practicing as creative artists, actors, singers, dancers, comedians, musicians, painters, sculptors, poets, story writers, fiction writers, astrologers, numerologists, palmists, vastu experts, yoga instructors, spiritual teachers, spiritual healers, spiritual gurus, religious teachers, religious gurus, doctors, therapists, physicians, psychiatrists, scientists, engineers, researchers, analysts, explorers, astronauts, pilots, aeronauts, ocean explorers, scuba divers, fishermen, professionals dealing in fishing industry, shipping industry, airline industry, hotel industry, travel industry, movie industry, music industry, television industry, book industry, media industry, teaching industry, coaching industry, consultancies, matrimonial services; and many other types of professions, depending on their overall horoscopes.

Let's look at some other facts associated with this nakshatra. Revati is considered as a balanced and tender nakshatra. It is considered as a female nakshatra. Vedic astrology assigns Shudra Varna and ether element to Revati. The Gana assigned to Revati is Deva and the Guna assigned to it is Sattwic. It is a level nakshatra and its Yoni or animal symbol is Elephant.

Contact Details

Website
www.AstrologerPanditJi.com

Facebook
https://www.facebook.com/HimanshuShangari

Email IDs
himanshu1847-himanshushangari@yahoo.com

himanshu1847-astrologerpanditji@yahoo.com

himanshushangari1847@gmail.com

16975817R00123